Forex Trading For Beginners & Stock Market Investing For Beginners

By

Tiernan Moore

Forex Trading for Beginners

Best Forex Trading Strategies to Make Money Today! Learn Forex Day Trading Secrets & Beginner Strategies To Make Money Currency Trading!

By Tiernan Moore

Chapter 1: Trading or Investing? Learn the Difference.

What is the difference between investing and trading?

To trade or not to trade: that is the question. Stock markets, day trading, traders, brokers—I know all of these can be a bit overwhelming, so let us first go back to the basics by starting off with breaking down the mechanics of stock market trading.

Trading, at the most fundamental level, is the exchange (i.e. buying and selling) of goods and services exclusively with the goal of making a profit—composed primarily of the buyer who demands the product and the seller who supplies the product.

In the context of the stock market, the buyer can either be an investor or a trader, and the main commodities that dictate all exchanges are called the securities, which are any form of financial assets that can be classified into three types, with the most common one (and the focus of this book) being the stocks. Typically, a trader has knowledge of these trends and possesses the skill to analyze the real-time or short-term performance and statistics available to come up with sound decisions—which are all achieved through regularly monitoring the existing patterns of the ever-changing market. On the other hand, an investor focuses on the particular stocks they want to put their money in and commits to learning the complex inner workings of the businesses they want to finance, with having long-term growth and profit in mind.

Later in this chapter, you will learn how to be in the shoes of both an investor and a trader, which will aid you in developing a clear perspective about stock market trading—at least on a surface level.

In a regulated stock market, you have to be a registered and an active member to be able to trade securities—specifically stocks. This means that an individual or a brokerage firm will typically perform the trading duties, and all of the services associated with it will be done by them in behalf of their client (you), which costs a certain commission rate for these services.

Throughout the years, the means through which stock market trading is done has drastically shifted from the traditional on-site trading (i.e. floor of New York Stock Exchange) to electronic trading, which can be accessed through a stem of portals and websites.

In contrast, investing is a transaction that involves shelling out a specific amount of cash and putting into a certain project or a platform with the goal of making a profit. In the context of the stock market, investing is done through having your money circulate across various platforms and letting them accumulate long-term profit through interest and appreciation of market value. Some of the more common types of investing are done in banks, stocks and bonds, commodity bonds, mutual funds (which let you "pool" your money along with several other investors at the same time), real estates, and start-ups. For these reasons, investing in larger platforms requires a lot of diligence and comprehensive research. You need to know which one is going to generate a bigger profit without having to take a lot of risks.

Aspects of Investing Behavior

Let's look below at the aspects of retail or market performance that will explain how trading and investing are polar opposites.

Exchange Duration This is the amount of time designated to an open placement in an industry, and it is one of the most crucial contrasts between trading and investing. Trading can take up as fast as a few seconds (depending on the change in the value of stocks in real-time), but investing typically takes months, years, or even generations to achieve significant financial maturation.

Recurrence Typically, for an average person in the market, trades happen much more than investments. Various types of trading can carry out thousands of transactions per session, while the standard investment approach may integrate simply a few transactions per quarter or even per year.

Relevance or Point of Observation The point of observation by which the industry is perceived is probably the biggest contrast between trading and investing. Traders commonly observe the market in terms of only the current trends and real-time statistics, while investors analyze stock behavior and growth potential on a much longer timetable.

Return of Investment (ROI) Depending on the resource market involved, the standard speed of ROI preferred by market brokers is around 6% annually. Investors, on the other hand, research to accumulate around 10% per month in order to generate a sufficient profit stream to cover living expenditures.

Chapter 2: Preparing Your Mind for Your First Trade

Get Your Mind Right for Trading

The concept of growing into a higher-level market trader is certainly not unintentional. Becoming good at anything—especially at trading—requires motivation, self-discipline, and tenacity.

You already have everything you need right at this moment to start trading. It's your mindset and willingness to learn that need to be developed.

Habits are formed out of routine. Now that you have identified your personal goals for trading, break down each one into its corresponding intent and strategies needed to achieve this (i.e. a schedule of activities).

Schedules have always been effective habit developers. They tend to influence your subconscious and result in your behaviors being somewhat robotic-like and perfunctory. Whenever this occurs with a good routine, it becomes natural to you to the point that you don't have to exert that much effort in sticking to it anymore. It's a clear win-win situation when you develop such habits out of schedules.

As frequently said by many, it is going to take you

21 days to create a new habit, and then you need to maintain that new habit for 90 days in order to create a lifestyle. Bringing your "A-Game' so that you can discover and initialize these mental resources is of fundamental value to your trading success. For instance, you need a sharp mind reinforced with a healthy blood glucose level as well as a hydrated and nourished body so that your built-in physiological network conveys cellular data successfully.

Aside from this, you need to be aligned in all areas of your life—physical, mental, and emotional behavior—in order to counterbalance common internal conflicts that often plague many people who trade. It is crucial for you to develop a highly effective morning routine intended to support your personal wellbeing. The main reason for this the susceptibility of beginner traders like you to lack of control. You need to stay in control by creating a daily schedule that you must adhere with religiously. Only by then can you truly establish the foundation for building the rest of your trading skills.

Here is an example of an effective routine that may benefit your whole structure (brain, body, and soul) in order to prepare yourself for the world of trading:

1. The example routine I am about to give you is a powerful tool for

addressing both your "mechanical data" and your "internal data." It is not enough to prepare only for the mechanical aspects (market information, news, and charts associated with price movements). You need to prepare your thinking, emotions, and behaviors before you become a forex trader. If you are having a bad day and can't fully concentrate on the work at hand, then you should take a day off from trading.

2. Begin your morning with physical exercise. Stimulate your body, oxygenize your circulatory system, and get the "spider webs" out of your mind and off your desk. I'm in no way talking about a full-blown work out (15—20 minutes of calisthenics and stretching exercise will do). Seriously, if you have not enjoyed the natural and organic high that happens from a disciplined routine of an early morning workout, then you do not know what you are missing out on. I promise you: it is relevant to your trading routine and is truly a healthy and stimulating experience overall, which will leave you radiant and self-confident throughout the day.

3. Consider a meditative workout to teach you how to be relaxed. As I have

mentioned earlier, this will definitely help you get in a totally aligned state so that you can be mentally aware, diligent, and centered with purpose. By simply relaxing and concentrating on your breathing, you will alleviate any immediate stress; focus your mind, body, and soul on nothing but the pure positive; and learn to be constantly aware of what truly matters at the moment.

4. Follow the plan. We will discuss creating a step-by-step strategy later—but once you have it, be sure to get rid of any doubt or personal bias. We all have them, and they can often get in our way when making important decisions. Be sure to review all of the graphs and charts that you want to refer to during your trading time. If you can, plan out in advance and pick the "play" you plan on using. Afterward, write down the reasons why you have chosen that, where is the entry point, what is the actual target, and when do you want to see a return on your investment. You will also need to factor in how long you want to stay in this particular market—essentially, your exit strategy. Pay attention to your instinct. It's powerful when trading. Don't ignore it.

This particular routine that I have given you is a prime example of how to balance both the physical and emotional aspects of trading. The only real chance any of you have at becoming an exceptional trader and building a reputation as a blue- blood is to make sure that you have the right mindset and are truly in touch with each of your intimate and non-intimate human capital. There are plenty of guides to teach you how to use subliminal and sentimental resources in order to continually create profit as a trader!

Patience Is a Virtue in Market Trading

I've had to put out missing and wanted posters for friends of mine who have dove into investing head first and have gone in with a "Las Vegas attitude." There are tons of articles, books, videos, and even commercials about which stock to trade and which platforms to use in order to suddenly "strike it rich" in the marketplace. Unfortunately, none of those truly has anything to do with any of us.

They have nothing to do with trying to help us navigate and have better success at trading as a newbie or even as a relatively more seasoned trader—it very much has everything to do with the almighty dollar. Think about entering a casino: the moment you walk in the door, you want to spend it all. It's the same concept with these corporations and brokerage firms. The idea is to merely keep you investing. That's not the case when it comes to trading.

Talk to some of the most successful traders out there, and the one common thing you will hear is that no matter how good you are, you can't "win" without having a little patience. People who sit down in front of slot machines at the casino want instant gratification—that's why it's not a good idea to have this mentality when trading. Hence, ditch that attitude right here and now.

Dennis Gartman, a well-established stock trader and author of The Gartman Letter, had this to say about the importance and underrated value of patience: "Proper patience is needed throughout the lifecycle of the trade—at entry, while holding, and exit."

What does it mean? Well, as a new trader, you are going to need to get used to patiently waiting for each of the sale prices of the stocks you want to trade to reach your "entry point" price. You cannot spin out of control if the trade you want all of a sudden has a price spike. It happens—get used to it.

What most beginners do is make the mistake of seeing the price immediately soar beyond their budgeted "entry point" price, and they panic. They let their emotions take over their better judgment and may often try to trade well above their intended bargaining power, just so they don't miss out. It's what many experts refer to as stock market FOMO (fear of missing out). In consequence, this introduces a greater risk of handing over some of their hard-earned cash and savings for an emotion-fueled judgment. How many of you have ever gone fishing? If you have, then you have yet another advantaged skill in trading.

The two bear the same concepts and principles. No matter what size the lake, pond, or ocean you are in, there is never too many fish for just one person.

Nobody, in fact, needs all of them or can do anything with that much. The point is: it's only necessary to go after those particular trades that you need and ultimately meet your personal profit goals.

There are tons of opportunities and trades in the market. It's not going to be hard to find opportunities. What will separate you from being successful from the opposite is the ability to find those trades that meet the trading criteria you have set and that also have good entry points. You may have been wondering what "entry points" exactly are. An entry point is simply the cost of the investment that you want to pay. It is typically the result of a planned-out strategy that is low on risk and high on the reward. It is an easy decision that doesn't require you to put any personal beliefs or emotions into it. It is the first step in being successful with your trades. There is plenty of information on the internet for you to learn more about trending entry points and even how to test out your trading ideas and concepts without spending any money. TradeStation is a great place to try a trading simulator risk-free before you actually invest real money. Give it a try!

Many successful traders are diligent when it comes to having complete patience and control of their emotions. This requires that you have self-confidence, do your research, and take care of your core (mind, body, and emotions). Nobody is perfect, but one thing that cream-of-the-crop traders do is they follow a disciplined routine, and they stick to it. No matter what they are feeling or going through at that moment, they do not falter from the plan, and they let their investments play out until the time is right. The important thing to remember is to not let your personal emotions control the trade—failing to do so leads to a loss and not a win.

With that being said, it is wise to keep in mind that you will have losses. It comes with the territory. It is your research on what good entry points are, your structured discipline and routine, and your knowledge of when to cut your losses that will result in a steady stream of profits and also help you avoid unnecessary losses. Stay the course, and let your routine and knowledge do the work. In doing so, you will be able to master the art of knowing when to re-analyze what is happening with your investment and when to sell your position.

What does that mean exactly? You are going to find yourself in positions where you have diligently followed your routine and remained disciplined—but despite your patience, you find that your investment has not moved in price or position. This then begs the question, "What do I do next? Do I remain calm and patient?" The short answer is yes. More often than not, you will find that by simply taking a deeper look at the investment and analyzing it, you will find out that maybe a certain financial factor has changed or that maybe your reason for wanting to enter the trade per se has changed. If you are able to determine after careful analysis that there is no valid reason for you to remain in the trade—then, by all means, sell it quickly. If just the opposite is true, and you find that nothing has changed, then it is a sensible decision to stay in your position.

While trading is about timing, research, analysis, and following a routine, it is rooted in mindset. This is what makes having patience a great virtue for exceptional traders. Do not confuse being bull-headed and stubborn with patience. The key is to follow your routine and your pre-set criteria to constantly improve your overall success with trading. One good thing is that you don't have to go through it alone.

Picking Out a Mentor to Work with

One thing you may want to consider when working in forex trading is the ability to work with a mentor. This person is preferably someone who already has experience in the market. If not, even working with someone who has done other forms of stock trading can make a big difference as well. This should be someone who can answer your questions, give you advice, and help you avoid some of the common mistakes that other forex trading beginners deal with.

Look around the industry and find someone who is willing to work with you. You may be surprised by the results. Many times people are thrilled that someone wants to get their advice, and they will be happy to help. Work with this person to learn the ropes of forex trading.

Your 3 Starting Factors to Success with Trading

We've talked a lot about the necessity for routine in order to be and remain successful as a trader, but it's more than that. It is also about analytical information and honing your skill set. One of the reasons that I have shared the history and even the story of Jesse Livermore is that at any point in history, including the major stock market crash, there was always some kind of sign or indication that pointed to bizarre patterns and pricing points. This is also useful now. As you analyze the trends and patterns, look to see what happened the day before. Were there any major spikes or drops in a specific trade? You must be able to evaluate what has consistently happened prior to the event and even after. This is a great indication for what you can expect in the coming days and the long-range direction of the marketplace.

For anyone to be successful at trading, you must seek to understand attested objectivity so that you can estimate what has happened and use that as the baseline for success. All expert traders are extremely adept at technological evaluation and analysis. How you develop that skill is to seek out

new opportunities to learn when the marketplace or
a particular stock trade has

performed completely opposite to what you have originally guessed. Look at each layer of the trade as if it were an onion, and peel back each layer to uncover the answers. Use them to help you develop your trading strategy and regimen. Nobody is born a successful trader—they become one. The 3 starting factors that all successful traders possess, develop, and follow religiously are as follows:

Approach

This is where you need to line up your trades with the established and tested self- restraint that allows you to follow what the marketplace is telling you.

Performance

Make sure that you are picking trades and following the patterns in the marketplace history and then basing your trades off of the good trends.

Plan

In order to get the best "entry point" price or buy-in price, make sure you are also looking at the technical aspect. This means evaluating the size of your current positions and when to quit to make sure that you are keeping a moderate level of risk at all times. When you do this, it permits a more transparent path for you to be able to see what lies ahead and to adjust quickly. Your individual trading routine and goals, even the way you capitalize on this day-to-day strategy, may be completely opposite of the way that I do it—but that only means that you will be able to see your own fortitude and fragility as a trader and not mine.

For example, in football, the coach and the players sit down and watch their own and their competitors' former games. This allows them to pause and stop the play to discuss what was good and bad about each play. Approach trading the same way. Score yourself on each of your trade approaches, performances, and plans. This is what will help you constantly learn and help you bring your A-game as a successful trader.

Chapter 3: Forex Trading Explained

Intro to Forex

Before we begin, you may want to have a marker so that you can flip back and forth between the terminologies (here's a quick link: Terminologies).

As you start this chapter, you now have the right mindset, a list of mentors you can reach out to, and awareness of the difference between trading and investing. You have even learned where you can do simulated trades without using your own money to give it a shot before starting in the real marketplace. Now, let's talk about Forex trading.

Just as I did when I first started out, I know you have tons of questions. Why do I need to care about London? What are these strange-looking numbers on my computer? What in the world is a pip? Am I going to fall asleep while I read this part? Can't I just Google this information myself?

While the answer to the last question is yes, there is a ton of information to sort through, and not a lot of them make any sense, are truly quite boring and monotonous, and most importantly, may not work for you and your lifestyle. This book is designed to help you sort through all the noise and learn how to trade and make a profit today while having a little fun in the process. By the time you are finished with this chapter, you will have gained a firm handle on the Forex marketplace and trading on the platform. Then, you will follow the simple step- by-step strategy to get started, and that's where the real fun begins!

Let's start with the least interesting part of the story, i.e. the history of how the Forex Market came to be. The only reason I need to mention this, as I did with the history of the stock market, is so that you have a solid knowledge library of the hows and whys in order to help you be successful.

In the year 1876, a monetary system called "The Gold Standard" or "The Gold Exchange Standard" came into existence as a way to preserve all of the currencies of the world by comparing them to the cost of gold. This meant that each piece of paper currency would have to be "backed" by gold. If you wonder why gold is not booming so much now, it is because of this decision. While I understand the concept of what regulators were trying to achieve, it only led to surges (up and down) in the price and value of gold, and it has leveled off at a downtick as of the start of the second world war. Countries in Europe had major difficulty keeping up with the cost of the war and printing money equivalent to

their ownership of gold. It wasn't good. Despite the
fact that we no longer base the dollar off of the price
of gold, gold has never managed to lose its
credibility as the preeminent value of the first form
of finance. The dollar bill would not be outdone,
though.

The United States ruled in favor of fixed exchange rates, which ultimately made the dollar the constitutional currency and the only currency in the world to be "backed" by gold. The "Bretton Woods System," as it was coined, would see its end in 1971 when the United States openly avowed that gold would not be exchanged equally for dollars.

In 1976, during the aftermath of the demise of the "Bretton Woods System," the widespread recognition of "floating foreign exchange rates" was gaining extreme momentum. This became the beginning of what we know as the Foreign Currency Exchange Market. The first trade using this electronic platform would not happen until late in the nineties.

So what is Forex exactly? In a glimpse, the Forex Market is a place where financial institutions, corporations, governmental agencies, traders, and venture capitalists can gather to play in the market and trade in currency. You will often hear the Forex Market referred to as the "FX Marketplace," "Currency Marketplace," "Foreign Exchange Currency Network," and "Foreign Currency Marketplace." This is considered to be the biggest and most easily accessible platform on the planet, and there are currently an estimated 4 trillion dollars in trades on the platform on a daily basis. This marketplace functions and operates Monday through Friday (24 hours each day), and the major markets are located in Japan, Australia, UK, London, France, Switzerland, and Germany.

It's nothing like the stock market where there is one central market, trade is regulated by the NYSE and is done "over the counter," and stocks are price-marked by every financial institution that all have varying degrees of price points. The concept of "Forex Trading" is where you and I come into play. We are considered market traders or also known as retail traders. We venture one currency against the other.

For example, if you believe (through your analysis) that the Japanese Yen will rise in value against the US dollar, then you want to purchase the JPY/USD "currency pair" when the price is low, if possible, and then you want to offload or sell when it is higher than what you have paid for (profit). Keep in mind that if by chance, you are wrong and that the US dollar does far better in the market than the Japanese Yen, then that's not a win. This is why evaluating risk vs. reward is critical when it comes to trading in general—and especially in Forex trading when dealing specifically with currencies.

For this reason, trading Forex is considered to be one of the most ideal and lucrative ways of life as compared to any other profession of its kind. Now, this is not an overnight process—please do not think that I am misleading you. If you stay grounded and focused, you will eventually get there. These are the main skills you will need to hone in order to help you gain profit from Forex trading.

Loss: You must be able to handle the losses without losing your head.

Self-Confidence: Trading losses smell fear like dogs do. Continually strive to push and to believe in your abilities and your strategies for trading successfully.

Commitment: You have to commit right from the start and stay the course.

Control: Keep a cool head at all times. Don't fall for the emotional traps and temptations that you will encounter.

Resilience: You have to be able to change course to profit and remain successful. Don't get so attached to an idea that you are too stubborn to do what needs to be done to win.

Concentrate: Do not get distracted from your goals and your trading strategy.

Rationale: You cannot use your emotions or personal beliefs to make trading decisions. Use logical reasoning and market trends to objectively evaluate the information and make informed decisions.

Framework: The framework is what keeps it all from falling like Jenga.

Patience: We talked about this in the last chapter. Learn when to stop, when to hold, and when to get out according to your strategy.

Authenticity: You have to realize that this is not the

latest get-rich-quick scheme. This is a living and breathing market that will either destroy you or make you. Your reality and understanding of that will determine your outcome.

Experience: Even as a newbie, you have a specific advantage to your trading that no one else has. Stay in tune with these special gifts and experiences that you have in order to analyze and profit from the market constantly.

Sensibility: Be smart, and don't go overboard with your trades and influence in the market. Be humble and sensible always.

As Forex traders, you have the ability to tap into the power and unpredictability of the market through research, understanding, and implementation of a solid trading plan/strategy, and then following it to a T with focused discipline and consistency.

Let's talk further about the mindset involved in Forex trading specifically. Key Points When Trading with Forex for The First Time

When starting out with Forex trading, many newbies find it easy to feel ignorant, flustered, and oftentimes even defeated and overwhelmed. There is a ton of information out there and even in this book. The best chance you have at success is to start out slowly and learn the key fundamentals about trading that come from experienced traders in the marketplace as well as from this beginner guide.

This is why we start with the basics. When I first started trading, I was a bit taken aback by all the information available. Had someone shared this information with me, I might have been a little bit better prepared mentally. Nonetheless, you get to learn from my experiences without all the pain. Pretty awesome of me, right?

So here's what you must not do: do not jump in with both feet without having any understanding, knowledge, or desire to learn about the market. In order to be successful at trading, you have to start with the solid foundation I've been talking about all the way up until now. Take the time to read the cheat sheet and all of the common trading terminologies in Chapter 7.

As a beginner, it's important that you not try to do too much at once. Learn a single trading strategy, as there are many, and stick with it. Learn it like the back of your hand. I will share a common trading strategy in the subsequent chapter so that you can have a great start. Before you try to learn a new strategy, master the one I'm going to share with you. Then, learn a new strategy and master that. Remember: there is no "magic potion" in trading, and taking unnecessary risks in hopes of striking it rich is what causes many traders to feel that false sense of joy and begin to think illogically and ultimately lose their profit. You will have some losses with trades; there is not a 100% win-win situation. Don't feel you have to jump ship. You have to have tough skin when it comes to trading and perfecting your discipline.

That's why you need to not get frustrated and upset with all of the different strategies and information that is out there as a newbie. All of us experts, at one point, were in your shoes—and it happens to the best of us when just starting out. Remember how we talked about finding a mentor earlier in the book? One of the best ways to avoid the stress of starting out as a trader is to partner up with someone who has had success in trading and someone who you can learn from. I do not recommend having a newbie as a mentor; you will just stress each other out unnecessarily.

Having a seasoned mentor will help you to not spazz out, as a beginner trader, and make unwise decisions when trades don't necessarily seem to be going the right way. Keep this in mind as you do the simulator trading expertise I suggested earlier—there's no real emotion involved because it is not real money. Hence, don't think you are a pro simply because you are able to keep your emotions in check during the simulator. The best thing you can do is to set up your stop losses in a justifiable position. What that means is that you have pre-established your personal risk and the dollar amount you are comfortable losing, in the event that happens. Once you do that, then set it and forget it. Let it do its thing. Remember: trading is not like watching the stock market. You absolutely do not need to do that with your trades. Check them daily, and leave them be.

Luckily for us, we have the internet and computers to help us out with staying in- the-know. Can you imagine being in the room when they were reading the "ticker tape" and writing out prices on the blackboard as we talked about during the early stages of trading and the market? Technology has allowed traders to simply focus on the price action and nothing else. It is a proven method that dates back to Japanese traders of rice when they used the candlestick method to determine the price of rice and where to sell and buy it. Do not get caught up in the overcomplicated and noisy data that is out there. It will only serve to infuriate you, frustrate you, and even worse, cause you to lose your profit.

While all of that may seem like a challenge, one of the biggest things you must avoid doing is being unrealistic with your expectations, your goals, and your lifestyle—especially when first starting out. If you run across someone telling you that you can retire or quit your job with a $500-trading account, they are misleading you and obviously have no idea how any of this works.

Yes, you can make a lot of dough trading with Forex. To get there, you will have to experience and overcome obstacles—the biggest one being yourself. When you stay realistic about the expectations and don't become starry-eyed with dollar signs, you tend to not risk as much. Nobody wants to add unnecessary risk to their trading.

Passive and sensible—that's how you win. I know it sounds stereotypical, but it is fact. When you trade with a high-speed fervor, you make yourself susceptible to that emotional baggage I've been working hard to get you to avoid. When you trade too much, you often make horrible mistakes that not only damage your self- esteem but also your account. When it comes to trading, less is more.

Once you learn how to analyze and read the data, view your resources to learn more about the charts and how to read them here: Charts for Forex Trading Beginners. When you have that down pat, then you learn the biggest one of all: when and where to put your stop loss. Do not put your stop losses too close to your entry point. It can backfire on you leaving a position too early or staying in it too long.

Lastly, this book is a great start, but it is only the beginning of your lifelong education. Do your homework, and be smart about investing your money. That's why it is important to manage your risk when taking part in Forex trading.

Money & Risk Management with Forex Trading

Risk management is a term that oftentimes makes the hairs of beginning trader's arms stand on end. Mine did the same thing. It is the first thing you must learn but is often the first thing ignored or even sadly forgotten in the training.

"It's not important if you are right or wrong. It's important how much money you make when you are right and how much you lose when you are wrong."– George Soros

There can never be a more poignant definition. In case you are not familiar with George Soros, he is an 87-year-old billionaire, philanthropist, and founder of the Open Society Foundations (OSF) NGO.

It is not at all as scary as it seems on the surface. It really is just a matter of using basic math when it comes to trade analytics. So let's begin with why it is even important when trading.

The gist of risk management is simply this: Get your position and the size right from the jump! What does that mean? It is the amount that you want to trade or that you are comfortable losing, which is going to determine your profits and the amount of risk you are willing to take.

You will often hear pro traders say "how much equation." They know that the size of the position is just as, if not more critical than the entry price point. Newbies often overlook this critical factor and go for those they think are going to make them instantly rich. That is the most dangerous approach one can take. So how do you get it right?

You have to learn what your individual goals are—not just saying you want to make money. We all do. That's too broad of an objective, and it doesn't discuss how you want to make money. Let's say you want to profit 10% a month. You will devise a strategy for trading and money management/risk to help you achieve that objective.

There are several main goals that each trader will have as a part of their strategy. We will talk about 5 of the most important objectives here, which are as follows:

1. ROI Objective: Determine upfront how much you want to make from each

of your trades. Do this on a monthly, daily, and weekly rollout. If you want, you can even do it for the entire year. It is all going to depend on your individualized approach.

2. Loss Objective: What is the most amount of money you can stand to lose

and not have to fold in the towel? What is the timeframe for that profit to occur? 3. Trade Volume Objective: What is the number of trades you are going to

invest in? Do this for each interval you set in
Number 1.

4. Risk vs. Reward Objective: What is your ideal profit margin on each trade?

If you can stand to risk 110 pips on that particular trade, but you want to be able to do a trade of 200 pips, then you are putting your risk for this trade at a 1-is-to-2 ratio.

5. Win Objective: This may seem like fantasy, but it is important to establish

how many of the trades you are making you want to win, how many you want to break even on, and how many you can stand to get wrong.

Trading for the sake of trading is not the best approach. When you have these clearly defined goals and objectives, it gives you a sense of accomplishment and something to aim for. Just as important as objectives are, you also need to understand when you need to pull out of a trade or not even get in, to begin with.

Experts always keep a well-defined plan and exit strategy ready in the event that their position does not go in their favor. This won't come to you overnight, though. It will take some testing and measuring to get it right, but here are a few tips when considering your loss and stop placement:

• Be sure to place your stop points at the right spot so even if the points take a hit, the strategy can still work for you. There are times when the trade is not going to work well, and if you don't add in these stop points, you may end up losing a lot of money in the process. These stop points protect your investment.

• It is best to not force your trade to have a good reward to risk ratio. Some traders try to do this with their stop loss. Doing this can result in more bad trades than before. Place it reasonably, and be sure it is within the market governance. If you feel that the risk vs. the reward on that trade seems to be too off for your comfort level, then do not get into that trade.

• Do not put stops and losses dead on any high or low position. Instead, focus on keeping it between 15-30 pips range. Trust me, you do not want to be stopped out on the high end nor the low end of the trading day.

• Make sure your exit plan is clearly laid out. You will need to do some testing and measuring to get this formula right for the profit you want to achieve. However, it is also wise to establish short-term profit, profit you want to let ride for a bigger payoff, and profit that you can let slide, even though not exactly perfect, but will still accumulate money.

The Basics of Calculating your Position

Size

Once you take the time to set your objectives as well as your goals in place and have laid out your exact exit strategy, then you want to focus on calculating your position size (see the definition by clicking this link).

To begin, use the calculator I have provided, or one you prefer, in order to determine the percentage of your trade profit that you are willing to risk on each trade.

To make this easier for a beginner trader, we have put together a formula that will help you out and you can add it to a simple spreadsheet, helping you to keep track of the whole objective for your trade. `

Link to Spreadsheet:
https://docs.google.com/spreadsheets/d/
1h04w3asCTVNY0D6EN9N6Sj5zGJDEOpoXBz1
RQsrRIYM/edit?usp=sharing

When you have calculated what your risk percentage will be, then you move on to determine the size of the trade.

Take the number of pips that you have between each of your entry points and between each of your stop/loss points. Put those figures into a calculator that can help you figure out your risks. Then, along with the trade balance, and your chosen percentage of risk that you want to take on, you can figure out the best trades to work on.

This calculator is a godsend. I wish I had access to it as a newbie. It literally determines the precise dollar amount it will take to buy each trade. You must get used to using some form of calculator, even if you don't use my suggestion, especially as you are starting out and just learning the value of all the different currencies in the marketplace.

$12,000 in GBPUSD will not have the same value as a $12,000 trade-in USDJPY. Using a calculator makes sure you are being as accurate as possible and doesn't require you to have a degree in mathematics.

This way, you achieve the success that you want without experiencing a lot of failures along the way. Getting right the "how much" of this step is critical to that. PIP Value Calculator (brought to you by 'Baby Pips'): https://www.babypips.com/tools/pip-value-calculator

The next thing you need to look at is leverage (influence) and how to control it. What that means is that the amount of leverage you enter a trade with is going to determine the "how much" you can purchase the trade for.

Let's say your trade account leverage is a ratio of 100:1. That means you can technically buy $100,000 worth of exchange per every thousand dollars you have available.

The most important thing I can tell you about leverage is that it is essential in regulating the number of trades one can have in their account at one time. The goal is to have a cap on the leverage limits you want to maintain on your trades.

If you decide to trade in the Forex Market using a broker, you need to understand that they have different leverage limits they allow any trader to have. Experts who do it on their own typically try to keep their leverage limits at a 10:1 ratio. That would be the equivalent of having $50,000 in trade values spread across five different trades. That's how you get the ratio of 10:1.

In order to set yourself apart from the average trader, you have to focus your strategy on reducing risk. Once you do that, then it is like a trickle-down effect. Everything else generally becomes easier to manage, analyze, and modify if necessary.

Diligently create the good habit of forecasting your position size through your clearly established objectives and goals.

Once you do this on a regular basis, it becomes like riding a bike. If you can get that down pat and remain consistent, then you, as a newbie, are already more informed and have a lower risk than about 90% of all the Forex traders in the world. Pretty cool, huh?

Forex Trading Analysis for Beginners

Why do you even need to know about technical analysis? The Forex market operates on a 24/7 basis. It never sleeps. Technical analysis involves looking at the documented price movement (both up and down) in order to determine what the price will be in the future. Once you become a pro and start using charts, technical tools and resources, and various Forex market indicators, you will find that this is the perfect way to make successful forecasts.

The two main considerations of technical analysis are:

1.) Trend Identification: this involves analyzing the ups and downs of the market through various graphs and even timespan.

2.) You must understand here and now that the only direction that a market can move is lateral—upwards and downwards.

Prices. on the other hand, move in a winding pattern, which means that it only has 3 categories of definition.

Sideways: This is simply a unilateral move in price, neither higher or lower.

Up-trend: When there is a winging upward of the price, also called "bull trend"

Downward-Trend: when the prices wind downward, also called a "bear trend"

What does all of this mean exactly? The technical analysis of the marketplace allows you to figure out not only the when and the where of getting in trades, but also when and where to leave them as well. It's based on a hypothesis and conclusions that the marketplace in general, is "helter-skelter." Nobody knows what will happen from one minute to the next, but the "price action" is not entirely arbitrary.

The Mathematical Chaos Theory is described as the proof that even during utter anarchy and disorder, there are verifiable trends that are destined to be repeated in the future.

To give this a real-world example, let's look at how weathermen/women forecast the weather.

No matter how much technical analysis you perform, no matter how many historical patterns you track, every single trader will tell you that there is no sure thing when trying to anticipate the movement of trade prices. So basically, you need to not think in terms of "good" or "bad" trades, but about the proper determination of your probable odds and then acting on them when the odds are on your side.

You must learn how to predict market trends and what direction they will go, when and where you will enter a position, and also the risk vs. reward ratio.

Keep in mind, that there is no one single magic formula or connection that is going to give you a leg up on trading. That's not how it works.

The keys to your success lie in not on a magic formula but in everything we have discussed you need up until this point: strategy, focus, and the ability to keep your emotions in check. It doesn't take a rocket scientist to get a few guesses right every now and then, but if you are not using proper risk management strategies, you cannot maintain a sustainable profit over the long haul.

Spotting Trends with Technical Analysis

Technical analysis used in Forex trading focuses on how the money moves. Is it moving up, is it moving down, or is it moving sideways?

When historical price levels are exceeded, missed, or created (low), then using a technical analysis tool or model will give you a solid suggestion on if you must go "long" or do a "short trade" regardless of the basic equity value of a specific currency.

Note: going long means you buy low and hope the price will rise over time. A short trade is when you buy, with no regard to the selling price, in hopes of selling it off and then buying back at an even lower price.

The 3 primary movements that make up the Forex Market are uphill trends, downhill trends, and lateral trends that don't move. So let's talk about those in more detail as it relates to risk management.

The lateral movement meaning is pretty literal. It states that the currency remains stagnant and is going to stay at a certain price for a set period of time. Expert traders will often create hand-drawn line graphs connecting the high points with the low areas of the price points. These will reveal the weaknesses or protection levels built into the marketplace. Some of the more common technical analysis tools will actually draw out the specific succession of the trends of the trades in order to estimate future patterns and opportunities.

The uphill and downhill patterns can be foreseen as a sequence of surges known as the first and second surge or "wave." The first surge is designed to steer the base currency price toward the straightforward trends in the market, and the second surge catches the ones that the first did not. It acts as a regulator if you will.

We've talked a bit about "currency pairs" at the start of this chapter. The most commonly used in the marketplace are GBP/USD, EUR/USD, and JPY/USD. These pairings set the trends, and they move rather strictly for a certain time period. Many attribute this to the way in which each of these countries is classified.

For the majority of trading's existence, USD, JPY, and CHF have been viewed as the world's refuge currency. The savior-of-it-all if other countries' currencies go to the crapper. It's also the basis for the majority of the trends we track and analyze in forex trading. This variety of currency trends and patterns allows traders, even beginners like yourself, to track and evaluate the movements of the different currencies and how they function.

Technical Indicators in Forex Trading

Even though the fundamental principle of technical analysis is based on trends and patterns in the marketplace, there are a number of different indexes that are used in determining what the price of a trade is going to be and how it will move (up, down, sideways) in the future.

There is even a great tool that identifies the potential for over-selling and over- buying, called Stochastics, which is an oscillator that tracks momentum.

There are even tools that are used by some traders that calculate the unpredictability of price, like Bollinger Bands.

No matter what technical analysis tool you end up using, they all have their own benefits and functionality—but the one thing that they all have in common is that they use previous data and price levels to determine risk.

Before You Begin Your Plan

Forex trading for beginners is extremely easy with the use of technical analysis and the help of all the experts who perfected it and have come and gone before you. It is a very integral part of your Forex trading strategy with lots of resources to back up claims of viability.

Use your better judgment about the tools you will use to help you analyze the data. There are tools like channels, trend-line trackers—you name it. They all function the same, regardless of the currency you are trading in.

Chapter 4: Confirmatory Factors to Help You Enter the Trade at the Right Time

In the trading strategies we are going to discuss in the later parts of this guidebook, there are going to be some confirmatory factors that you need to look for. These are important because they help you to use the graphs you have and confirm the information that you see. It is an added level of support that ensures you are entering and exiting the market at the right time to make a good profit or to limit your losses. The more of these confirmatory factors that you can find for a particular trade, the more secure it is.

Support and Resistance Levels

Support is a price level where you can expect a downtrend to pause because of the demand. As the price of a chosen security drops, the demand for these shares will increase because the security is lower in price. This forms the support line. Once this area has been identified, it can provide the trader with some good exit or entry points.

The reason for this is because as the price of a security reaches that resistance or support level, it can do one of two options. Either it will bounce away from this level, or it will violate the price level and continue in the same direction until it hits the next resistance or support level.

Most forms of trading will assume that these resistance and support zones are not going to be broken. Whether the price stops at these levels or breaks through them, traders will bet on the direction and then determine if they are right. If the security ends up going in the wrong direction, the trader can close the position, but it would be at a small loss. However, if the trader guessed right and the price moves in the right direction, the move could be large and they can make some good profits.

As a trader, you can use the various graphs and tools at your disposal to help you figure out when the resistance and the support are. Since many securities tend to stay around these points and don't often go above or below them, this can be used to help you make good guesses on the trade. When the security reaches the lower price point based on this information, which is a good time to purchase because you are getting the best price for the security. When it reaches the higher point of the support and resistance, you can sell and get a bigger profit.

This isn't always accurate, and you also need to combine it with big news events and other information. On occasion, the security will break past its support and resistance. Sometimes, this results in a large profit for you if you catch that change. But if it goes down, you could lose a lot of money as well.

Round Number Indicator

Round numbers are going to refer to numbers you see in trading that end in at least one zero. It is often done at levels like the 50 or 100 mark. Let's look at the AUD/USD currency paring that just broke up to $1.02. This one is going to be written out as 1.0200. The next level that it could break would then show up at the 50, which would put it at 1.0250.

This can be easy to use because the price of a forex option is often going to react during these specific levels. If you see that the figure will then coincide with some other proof points at that same level, such as support and resistance level, Fibonacci levels, or pivots, then it is likely that the price is going to react and turn at these levels as well.

Fibonacci Forex Indicator

A Fibonacci retracement is a good tool to use and many professional technical traders like to use it. This tool is one that will use some of the key numbers that were discovered by Leonardo Fibonacci. This number sequence is important because it shows you some important relationships that occur between the numbers in a series, and it will be expressed in the form of ratios.

During a technical analysis, this tool is then created when you take two points that are extreme to one another. These are going to be the major peak and the major trough on any chart you look at. Then you will take those major parts and divide the vertical distance and then you get the ratio that you are looking for. These ratios are 23.6, 38.2, 50, 61.8 and 100 percent. Once your levels are determined, you will draw out horizontal lines and then use them to help you figure out where the support and resistance levels will be. Why are these ratios used? Let's see a bit more about Fibonacci and how it works first.

The Fibonacci sequence of numbers is the following: 0,1, 1, 2, 3, 5, 8, 13, 21, 34, 55, 89, 144 and so on. Each of these numbers relates to each other because they are the two previous terms added together. One characteristic of this sequence is that each of the numbers will be about 1.618 times greater than the number that came before it. This relationship is common with all the numbers in the series and can be the foundation of using retracement studies and common ratios.

Another thing to note is that the key ratio of 61.8 percent is known as the golden mean or the golden ratio. This one is found by dividing one number in the series by the number that comes after it. For example, you would take 21 and divide it by 34 to get 0.6176. If you divided 55 by 89, you would get 0.6179.

To get the ratio of 38.2 percent, you will divide whichever number you choose in the series by a number that you can find if you look two places to the right of that number. So, if you started with 55, you would divide it by 144. This will equal 0.3819.

To get the 23.6 percent ratio, you will divide your chosen number by the number that you find in the sequence that is down three places if you go to the right. So, if you started with 8, you would divide it by 34. This gives you the number 0.2352.

While the reasons are not always clear, these ratios may seem random, but they are going to play a very important role when you are trying to do a trade in the stock market. You can use these ratios in order to help you figure out the important points that may cause your chosen asset to switch directions and go either up or down based on the current trend. You will learn that the direction of a trend you are following is going to continue as soon as the asset has time to retrace to the ratios that we have above.

When working in the stock market, the Fibonacci retracements are going to be used the most. This is because they are simple and can work with almost any type of trading instrument. These retracements are important because they can be used by the trader to help confirm the support levels and the resistance levels that you want to trade on and can be used for counter trend trading.

Forex Trends

For many securities, you will be able to look at the data that is put on a chart and see the general direction that the currency is heading. Hopefully, the trend is going up, but the data could show that the price of the security is going down, or even staying pretty steady. Either way, you can use the information that you see in the trend to help you make decisions about when to purchase and when to sell your securities.

There are three main types of trends that a security will follow, and it is likely that a security will go through each type many times during its lifecycle. These trends include uptrends, downtrends, and sideways or horizontal trends. The first two are pretty easy to understand, but the third one is going to occur when the movement in price is so minimal that the line pretty much looks like it is going straight rather than up or down. Sometimes the sideways trend is just known as the security not having a well-defined trend, either going up or going down.

Along with the different types of trends that we talked about above, you will soon notice that there are three different classifications of a trend. These have to do with for how long that particular trend is going to take place. Sometimes the trend is long-term and this is a good indicator that it will keep moving in that same direction, probably at a similar rate, for the foreseeable future. The trend can also become an intermediate trend or a short-term trend. When you are looking at currency pairs in forex trading, a long-term trend will often have a few other trends, specifically an intermediate trend, inside to make it work. that push it along, and short-term trends can be components in both the intermediate and the major trends.

In this, you also want to take a look at the trendlines. This is a technique to use in charting where a line is added to the chart to help you see what trend is showing up in your chosen currency trend. Drawing a trendline is not difficult, you just add one in to show off the general trend a bit. Since there is often a lot of ups and downs when looking at the price movements, this line can give you a general idea of where all those ups and downs are going overall.

When you are picking out the security that you want to invest in, you definitely want to look at the trends it has followed. This gives you a good idea about

whether the market is good for that security and if
you will actually see the price go up.

Chapter 5: Specific Forex Trading Strategies to Earn a Profit Today!

I hope by now you have realized that it doesn't take years of learning, or even any background in finances in order to have success with Forex and creating a solid plan of action. Now it all boils down to the strategies and how to get this party started!!!

To get up and running with Forex you will need three things: 1. Trading Account (Forex Only) 2. Some moolah, cash, dough 3. Being a great predictor and analyzer of trends and then being able to adjust your strategy

It's really a matter of guessing which country's currency value will change vs. another countries. You can make two guesses, one that says you believe Country A will rise over country B, just the opposite. You set the countries you want to make predictions on, you set the time frame that the value movement will occur.

If you chose to see country A's value rise above country B's and it actually does as you predicted it would, when the trade is closed or is done, then you win and have some money to spend! Let's dive in to the specific steps to get you on the path to making a profit with Forex...today, and then on to the strategies when you have the housekeeping out of the way!

Step 1: Open Your Account on Forex In order to be able to trade on the Forex marketplace, you will need to have a Forex approved trading account. You can do so here at Forex.com brought to you by the Gain Capital Group. (https://application.forex.com/en-us/step/1)

It takes less than 5 minutes to create your account as a beginning trader, and this site even lets you try a risk-free demo version before you actually invest in the real marketplace. I referred to this as a simulator in earlier chapters.

Here you can download the popular MT4 platform which has excellent charts.

Another platform I recommend used by professionals is Bloomberg. Although this platform is not necessarily cheap, it will definitely set you apart from the 90% of people who fail or quit trading forex. It is great at keeping up with live events and for getting advice on your decisions.

I strongly suggest you get a demo account before you open your regular account so you can see it live in action as you go along. You can test drive all of the features of the actual trading platform and you

will be given a specific number of credits on the
house, if you will, with no risk. If you want to keep
going beyond

the initial allotment of credits, you can purchase more and keep training yourself on the demo account. Once you feel you are ready to come down off the porch and join the big dogs, then you can go over and open your regular Forex trading account.

Step 2: Pick Your Trades When you are test driving around in the demo account, hopefully you have followed my suggestion, before creating a regular account, it is quite common for beginning traders to just haphazardly pick your trades without any planning or thought put into what currency pairs you are selecting or even why you are pairing those two against each other.

This demo time is the only time you get to be so loose with your currency pairs without any regard to the principles. In a regular account it's not monopoly money you are trading with your real, hard earned cash and you MUST take the time to understand and learn the currency pairings. You can find a resource for that in the next chapters.

Forex trading, as mentioned revolves around the ability to determine which country's currency value is going to see movement. That means knowing which one is going to go up and which one is going to go down. Your predictions coming true are how you make money, and for that very reason I recommend that you start to look on your own for the resources and handy tools that will help you to make the predictions on which one is going to fail versus which one is going to rise.

Many of these tools are available to you, for free on the web. I am not endorsing any one tool in particular as I want you to choose the one that feels right and works best for you and your style. Simply Google "currency pair prediction tools" and you will get millions of results. For now, put a pin in that. You have your demo account, you've played around with it, now what?

Step 3: Get Your Money's Worth You don't buy a house off of Craigslist without first seeing it, and you don't buy a car without taking it for a test drive. Well at least most of us don't anyway. The same holds true when shopping around for a credible broker or platform to sign up on.

The broker you choose should have experience working with beginner traders and come with a real value proposition that will benefit you as a new client.

The numbers and statistics on people literally making a decent amount of money with Forex is readily available. If you are looking to get rich quick, without any work, this is definitely not for you. Luckily for all of us though, technology and ease of access to information has made it possible for just about anyone, even your aunt who doesn't know how to turn on the computer, how to become a successful Forex trader, and actually earning a profit.

It wasn't always that way. When Forex first hit the market, you had to have bank. No literally, you had to basically be a bank and have large capital and/or assets that would buy and hold large amounts of one country's currency and then convert it to the original currency and sell it. Whew.

Luckily, we don't have to worry about all of that. You need an account, a broker and access. Let's go!

Step 4: Choose Your Currency Pairs Now, as Forex traders, we simply go into a trade on one or possibly two, as a beginner, trades on two country currency pairs. One country's currency value movement over another, remember that.

That means you have to decide which two countries to pair out and determine which one you think will go up in value, which ultimately means the other goes down.

To decide which pairings to make before you enter a trade, you will be given a chance to choose a broker who is experienced in the currencies you set as your preference on your account. It's typically the USD for those of us here in the United States. When you are using your regular account, you are free however to pair up any two currencies, not just your home currency exchange.

For instance, even if we have the US dollar as our home currency, we can still pair up two different countries other than the US.

Step 5: Determine Your Profit Regardless of what platform you ultimately decide to trade Forex on, you must make sure that they have the ability to display your "gain" potential next to each pairing to help you make an informed decision. There is no set rule when determining this "gain" and it is important to note that broker commissions will ultimately affect your profit margin so do your due diligence in what that difference is among the top platforms and broker houses.

Step 6: Set Your Trading Period & Exit As we close out this chapter I want you to remember that no matter what choices you are presented with in terms of how long you let a trade stay live, you must evaluate when you want to exit a trade and when to stay. A common terminology you will hear can be attributed to Kenny Rogers, "Know when to hold'em and Know when to fold'em."

You will soon become familiar with hearing the term "day trading". That simply means that on any given day, a Forex trade can be performed on the market and closed on the exact same day it's opened. You are not by any means, obligated to keep your trades that short, you can choose to have them close in whatever interval you want. It is just common practice for beginning and even some expert traders, to have trades that are going to close on the same day, which allows them to make a profit they can then re-invest for a longer trade.

I'm going to show you how you can put your own Forex trading strategy together for effective day trading. We will also determine your stop loss and winning goal, so you start off on the right foot.

As we go through this information, I want you to keep in mind the founding principle of Forex. That's to profit, obviously, but also knowing how much you stand to win or lose as both are quite possible. Pay special attention to the next section, this is what is going to help you generate that profit today.

By following this step by step strategy, I am quite certain that anyone without any trading experience, or FX market experience, you are going to be able to make a quick and even long-term sustainable profit.

Be sure to do your research and use your resources

to understand in depth the currency pairs, loss and stop placement, and your position size.

Step 7: Start with Determining Your Pairings You will want to have some knowledge about the options of pairings you have, and which ones you want to begin trading with. This is going to be the case with any trade you do in the Forex marketplace. This does require you do some extensive research, so you understand in-depth what it takes to make a currency rise or fall over a certain amount of time.

I select my currency pairings by trying to guess correctly, based on country stats and information that is released by the government and other credible sources, and most importantly, the "economic calendars" that each country releases.

What this is, is a specific day and time that the largest countries around the world release data that reveals how well their stocks did in various categories.

Step 8: Decide When You Want to Close Out As I mentioned, there are plenty of trades that have an opening and closing span of one day. After you decide what currency pairs you want, it is time to decide how long you want to keep your trades active and live on the market.

You can even lock in and place a 60 second trade.

That means you choose your pairing, you choose 60 seconds as your expiry time, and you either win or lose at the close of that trade. This is not like analyzing the reports and country data like I do for longer term trades, these are your quick and small money makers to get your feet wet, or as I mentioned, simply help fund your future trades.

Step 9: Set your Loss and Win Targets Regardless of whether you are doing your own trading, or using an individual broker, you will need to determine when you want to set your stop/loss and win targets before you begin trading. These are essentially guided by how much money you have to trade, but there are also other things to consider as well.

As you start out, keep your stop loss targets based on the value of your trades and within no more than 10% max of your entire budget you've established for trading. This will also be your winning target, or profit percentage.

Let's give an example. Let's say you want to trade $200 a day and that is what you have budgeted, that is your goal you are sticking to it. If you want to make $30 on that trade, then that is essentially your stop loss target. So, if a trade you enter increases by that $30, then you want to lock in that price, and profit and immediately close the trade.

On the contrary, if you lose that $30.00 over a series of trades, or even on one single trade, your budget drops by $30.00 so you want to stop all trades for that day and you will log a loss in your journal and trade logs.

Step 10: Plan for Long Term Profit Also In order to make long term profits in Forex trading, you will need a good 4 to 6 months. This includes your learning time, becoming a master of the different strategies in Forex trading using charts, you've worked your demo account to death and you are ready to go into a real trade with a deposit of $550.00.

Your average profit will be between 15-20% which is the market average, and you will have essentially doubled your initial deposit by the end of the third month. I earned my first grand in seven months of trading. Please note, remember, I didn't have the resources you have available to you in this book, so your results will typically be faster than mine, depending on how fast acting you are. Also, if you want to do this quicker, you run the risk of losing it all. Instead of rushing through trads, take your time, and get a good sense for how the marketplace moves and how to interact with others on it. There's nothing more satisfying than watching your money grow over time.

Step 11: My Recommended Strategy Since this is a book for beginners, I HIGHLY HIGHLY recommend you start out by focusing on one

currency pair. This will allow you to "master" that
pair and make your life much less complicated
starting out.

If you need a recommendation, I suggest starting out with the EUR/USD. Don't quote me on this, but this currency pair makes up about 75% of all forex trades and is by far the most popular currency pair traded.

Now the following is a day trading strategy and is not for everyone, but I like to trade the EUR/USD on the 5 and 15 minute charts. Try this on the demo account you set up and you may be surprised at the results!

I just had a friend with zero experience, try out the demo account at Forex.com. Using this strategy he profited 18 cents on his demo account in 5 minutes! Obviously 18 cents is nothing to write home about, but for his very first trade ever, with no experience, I'd say that's pretty good!

See Forex Trading Doesn't Have To be That Hard !

Resources & Valuable Links

Below are some links to further your research and training. Check these out, but also do your own research so you are well informed.

Learn about Stop Losses and How to Set Them: "Stop-loss in Forex is critical for a lot of reasons. However, there is one simple reason that stands out - no one can predict the exact future of the Forex market. It does not matter how strong a setup may be, or how much information might be pointing to a particular trend. Future prices are unknown to the market and every trade entered is a risk." https://admiralmarkets.com/education/articles/forex -basics/

what-is-stop-loss-in-forex-trading-and-how-to-set-it

Stop Loss Calculator: "FX Calculators that work out the pip value of each position in your chosen currency, as well as our Currency Converter and cTrader Commission Calculator are all vital for Forex traders."

"FxPro also has a mobile app available for both Apple and Android devices, which includes all these CFD Calculators to help you trade on the go." https:// www.fxpro.co.uk/trading/calculators/stop-loss-take- profit

Research Currency Pairings: The Ultimate Cheat Sheet: "You would never buy a house without understanding the mortgage, right? Yet when it comes to the Forex market, many traders forget to familiarize themselves with the currency pairs they're buying and selling."https://dailypriceaction.com/forex- beginners/forex-currency-pairs

Learn More about Expiry Times: "After choosing high or low, picking the right expiry is the hardest thing for traders to decide. Several factors can impact which expiry is the right one. Failure to pick the right one can often mean the difference between an option closing in or out of the money. " https://

www.thatsucks.com/60-seconds-1-hour-30-minutes-choosing-the-right-binary- options-expiry/

How to Decipher Forex Charts: "When you have a certain amount of experience and proficiency in currency trading, it would be a good decision to discuss the tools which Forex traders regularly utilize. Owing to the leverage and the fast-paced nature available in FX trading, a lot of Forex traders do not hold particular positions for a very long time period." https://admiralmarkets.com/education/articles/forex-basics/how-to-read-forex-charts

Most Frequently Used Chart Patterns in Forex: "With such a huge variety of ways to trade currencies, selecting the most common methods can save a lot of time, money and effort. By using popular and simple approaches a trader can design a complete trading plan using Forex trading chart patterns that frequently occur and can be easily spotted with a little practice. Charts, including Ichimoku and candlestick patterns, can all provide you with visual clues on when the best time to trade is."

https://admiralmarkets.com/education/articles/forex-analysis/ most-frequently-used-forex-chart-patterns

Now we will focus on specific technical analysis strategies you can use to trade forex and make some money!

Chapter 6: Forex Trading Strategy 1 – The Bladerunner Trade

The Bladerunner is a strategy that is going to use pure Price Action to help the trader find entry points. You will use support and resistance levels, round numbers, pivot points, and candlesticks to make this work. You don't need to work with any off-chart indicators or indicators that appear below the chart window in their own window, but you can include one if you want that for a bit of extra confirmation. This strategy can be traded almost any time of the day, but there are some times that are better and more reliable than others. For example, many forex traders will use this strategy when the Asian session opens because it gives them a decent break out point to rely on.

First, we need to look at the entry for this particular strategy. The essential parameters for this setup would be:

The price needs to break out of the consolidation or a range prior to entry. This means that it must be trending. The price must then retest with the 20 EMA successfully

If the price is about the EMA at the time, then it

must bounce from and then stay above this EMA to be a good trade. The same is true if the price is below the EMA. To be more specific here, the first candle that touches the EMA should be close on the same side of the EMA as it approached it from.

When this happens, it is going to be your signaling candle. The price has now rejected the EMA and we are going to check to see if the next candle will confirm what we just saw. If the next candle does move away from our EMA, then it confirms our information. This is a simple way to check what is going on with the trade and to see if this strategy will work or not. As a beginner, if you want to be a little more on the safe side, you could wait for a recognizable forex pattern to occur and then work on the trade.

Some things that you should remember with this particular trading strategy include the following:

You want to always check for a confluence of reasons to enter your trade. For example, it is always a safer idea to have more than just the rejection of your 20 EMA. Ideally, you would want to see this happening at the same place of the resistance level, the pivot level, or another price impact point that is big. Always look for any news announcements that may come out when you use this strategy, especially when the numbers are on the lower end. This

can make a difference in whether the trade will continue in the same manner or not. Some traders recommend not entering into a trade half an hour or so before a news event that is scheduled, and then they wait after the news is released before they consider their trade. This helps to steady out the market a bit before entering. Always trade in the same direction of the current trend. You can find this based on which side of the EMA the trend is on. There are other strategies that will have you go against the trend, but this is not one of them.

There are several different approaches that you can take when doing the Bladerunner strategy. But the one we are going to use here is to open up two orders to make it work. This can increase your potential profits and can decrease your potential risks. The orders that you should do to make this strategy successful include:

For a long entry:

To do this one, do two stop orders. You want to place these with an entry that is two pips above the confirmatory candle. The orders need to expire at the beginning of a new candle. For example, if you are entering these orders on the five-minute chart, these orders are going to end when the next five-minute candle starts. You can then place a price action on the next five-minute candle to keep it going. You can place your stop loss two pips below the signal candle. This is not something that is set in stone, but it is a good thing to follow if you need some help. You can place the stop behind a swing point if that one will provide you with a better stop size. To set your take profit on the first order, you should make sure it is set to the amount that is equal to your risk in pips. So, if the risk here is 20 pips, the profit target should be set at 20 pips. To set your take profit on that second order, you will want to double your risk in pips. So, looking at the previous example, you would want to set the second order take profit around 40 pips.

For a short entry

For this one, you will take two sell stop orders and then place the entry two pips below the candle you used for confirmation. The orders for this one are going to expire when a new candle starts. For example, if you again enter with a five-minute chart, these orders will end when that five-minute candle is done. This is true unless you have already filled out a price action on the new candle. You can place the stop loss two pips above the signal candle. Again, you can do it behind a recent swing point if that is going to give you a better stop size here. For your first order, the risk needs to be equal to your risk in pips.

For the second order, you will set the risk at double your risk in pips.

Once you have seen that the price is moving in favor of your trade by an amount that is equal to the initial risk, then one of the orders will need to be closed. This is because it reached the take profit at the first level. Then the stop loss that is on the other order will be moved up to the breakeven point. This helps you to at least break even on the trade, but hopefully still make a profit.

The order that is left will be placed at that breakeven point until the market automatically closes up that trade. This will happen either by reaching your profit target or because it stops out when the trades reaches the breakeven. At times, you may avoid this rule if you feel that there is a news announcement that is about to come out and you think it will have a positive influence on the profits you make.

Chapter 7: Forex Strategy 2 – Daily Fibonacci Pivot Trade

The next strategy we are going to look through for forex trading is the daily Fibonacci pivot strategy. This method is going to use the Fibonacci retracements with the daily pivot levels to help you figure out the right entries for your trade. You can use the parameters anywhere that you want, but a good place would be the 38 and the 50 percent.

There are different interpretations that come with this option, but we are going to use the following steps to help us win with this strategy:

Lok for an entry point. You want to look for a pair of currencies where the average true range has been above the trading session for the previous day. Preferably, you want a currency pair where this has occurred for at least the past five days to know you have a strong pair. Some things that you should look for include:

o Look at where the stock ended as a high and a low the day before. If you see that the price shows up above the current central pivot, then you get to draw a fib on the chart. o From the high and low of the previous day, if the price ends up

being below that point, then you can draw the fib. You can then take some time to see if there is any confluence in those levels of retracement that you find. Use the pivot from the daily central to see if this works. If you see that the price retraces to the confluence identified, then it is time to enter at market. Or you can choose to wait it out for a confirmatory candle signal to help make it a little safer. It is a bit riskier to jump in without getting that confirmatory signal, but it does increase your reward to risk ratio and can give you more profits.

This may be confusing, so let's take a look at a few charts to see how this strategy is going to work:

For this first chart, we will look at an example of how you would do your long entry. The retracement is going to be at 38 percent, and we are also looking at the daily central pivot.

With this example, you could technically enter the market either way. You could purchase at the first touch of that particular level, or you could wait it out and see if the morning star candle formation shows up. Both of these entries, at least in this example, would give you a potential target at 127 percent Fibonacci extension, which is easily reached.

The stop loss that is recommended for these trades is one level from where you would like to have this trade occur. With this example, we are going to focus on having a retracement level that is at 50 percent. We also would recommend throwing in a few pips extra to have some safety room.

The next trade is going to show the reverse setup that you can do on the previous trade. We are going to do the sell when we reach the retracement level of 38 percent.

This one is a good example because the set up because there is a big drop, for some reason, that occurred the day before in the trading session. This drop shows that there was a change in sentiment with other traders, which would have added in some weight when the trader was trying to sell the security.

Chapter 8: Forex Trading Strategy 3 – The Bolly Band Bounce Trade

As a new trader, you will find that trading on an obvious trend is a much easier process compared to trading when the price seems to be range bound, or when the price appears to be moving sideways. Many beginner traders will actually pass on even trading in this market because they want to see some trends to help them determine if it is the right time to purchase or sell the security. If you are ready to try out something new and see some great profits, then there are a few strategies that you can use when the price range or the price movement seems to be more restricted for the market. The Bolly Band Bounce is one of those strategies you can choose.

This strategy is based on the behavior of price that the trader observes were the Bollinger bands are going to be the factor that forms your short-term price limits. With the example above, we will see that the Bollinger bands are going to exhibit elasticity, similar to what you would find in a rubber band. The price is going to approach the outer band, but there is going to be some resistance and they snap back over. You will see this if the trend doesn't vary far from the central point, especially for longer periods of time.

You can make use of this kind of behavior in the market, but you have to be quick and you have to know how the market works with these kinds of trades. The way that a trader is able to use this type of behavior is to watch the bounces that occur on those outer bands. This strategy would not be that effective when you are in a market with a lot of sharp trends. But if the market seems to be in a range, it can work for some short-term scalps and can ensure that you are still going to make some money, even without some major trends going on.

The first thing that we are going to do when you see this kind of strategy is to check that your chosen company or stock is actually going to stay in range. Remember that this strategy isn't going to work that well if the security isn't actually staying in that range at all. There are several ways to check and see if the security stays in a range, but one of the simplest methods is to check whether or not the price is going to stay on one particular side of that mid-line that you draw. If you are able to draw a straight line that goes through the price points, and the price either stays on or on one side of that line, then you have a range.

If you see that this is true, and the price is consistently making lower lows than that mid-point, then the price is trending down. The opposite is going to apply to the uptrend. If you see that the price ends you staying above that mid-band, and it makes highs that are higher than before, then you are looking at a security that is in an uptrend.

The illustration below is going to show a price in a downtrend. Then, as it moves to the right, it changes into a ranging market:

Looking at the circle at the bottom of the chart, you will see a signal that the security is about to turn from a trending market to a ranging market. This shows that there is a tweezer bottom candlestick pattern has begun to show. The signal is going to be stronger if it occurred at the same time as a Fibonacci retracement level, a significant pivot level, a round number or a support and resistance.

You can choose to trade at this level if you would like. Many traders choose to wait to get a confirmation that the price is really ranging by a turn at the opposite band. This helps you to make sure that you are actually in a range at the time so that you can get a bit more security when you are setting up your trade.

Now that we understand a bit more about how this particular strategy works, it is time to set up your take profits, stop loss, and entry limits. Before you do this though, it is important to know that this strategy is basically a strategy for scalping with forex. This means you want to enter into the market using this strategy right when the signal is confirmed in the market, using an aggressive stop loss, and then take the profits when the opposite Bollinger band shows up.

Once you have been able to confirm the move in price, you should move the stop loss over to breakeven as soon as possible. If you fail to do this, you might get caught in a pattern of price bouncing at the mid-band, and then you have to retrace in order to take out that stop. This could happen in the first trade we had above if you didn't move over to the breakeven right away when it was safe to do so.

With this strategy, you will have to take your time and use your own judgment to figure out when it is safe to move over to the breakeven. If you do it too early, you are going to be stopped out by some normal retracements, even if your price moves in the direction you wanted. This one will take a little bit of time to get used to and experiment with.

One final thing to note with this strategy is that it is going to work the best when the market is quiet and there aren't any big news announcements that are about to come out on the pair that you want to trade in. it is also helpful if the pair doesn't give in to spiky price action. You want to look for confluence at the outer band rather than just entering a trade just because it looks like the price has reached a chosen outer band.

Chapter 9: Forex Trading Strategy 4 – The Forex Candlestick

Candlesticks are great strategies to go with no matter what kind of trading you want to work with. They can really show you the trends that are going on in the market for that security, and you can adjust the methods to work no matter what kind of market you enter. There are actually quite a few different types of candlestick strategies that you can work with, and we will take a look at a few of them below:

The Double Top

This kind of candlestick pattern is going to form after there is either strong bullish conditions or a strong price rally. It is easy to define because of the double top patterns kind of looks like two mountain peaks that form into an "M" shape on your chart: An example of what you are looking for in your graphs when using the double top strategy includes:

These two peaks will generally show up because they are reacting to strong resistance that shows up in the market. the initial bullish wave is going to hit the point of resistance before it does a bounce right away. It can then find a bit of support again.

Eventually, the bulls of the market are going to pick up their steam again. This results in the market pushing that stock up to a higher price. Then the market will be able to retest that resistance level. Often the bulls are not going to have enough strength to control the market for long and the price ends up doing a bounce again to help make that second peak.

The best way to trade when you see the double top candlestick pattern for the trader to watch some of the charts and wait to see that second peak start to form. Then you can do some price breaks that are short and happen below your neckline.

The Double Bottom

The next type of candlestick that you can use is known as the double bottom. This kind of candlestick pattern is the inverse of what we did with the double top pattern. It is going to form when you see a strong bearish move and it will have more of a "W" shape to it compared to the last one. An example of what this would look like in the market is the following:

A double bottom is going to signal there the bears of the market are exhausted. This gives the bulls time to take control at that support level. Now the bears of the market are able to move the prices so they go back down to the stocks support level. At some point, the bulls are going to try and drive that price back up. Because the bulls are rejecting this support, they are going to create that first V shape. The bears are going to work on fighting the bulls and driving the price of the stock back down.

When the bulls and bears fight and the market gets back to the support level that second time, the bulls are going to be the winners again, at least for a bit, and they work to drive the prices back up again. This results in another V in the chart. This final move will help finish this pattern.

Head and Shoulders

The head and shoulders strategy is another candlestick pattern that works on exhaustion. This one is not always the most reliable because it forms after the market has been trending in a certain direction for some time. As the name suggests, the candlestick pattern is going to have a head and ten two shoulders. The pattern shows up when the bulls find a good resistance level, retrace themselves back, and then find support, which can create the left shoulder. At this stage, it can be impossible to tell if the head and shoulders pattern is going to form until later.

When the bulls start to try and gain some strength here and push the price of the security up again. The last resistance line that you tested on the chart is going to be broken through with this. But these higher prices are not ones that the bulls are able to keep with, and the price will go back under the resistance due to this false break. The false break is going to create the head part of this pattern.

With this pattern, the bulls are going to fail in their quest and they won't be able to maintain the prices that fall above your resistance level. When this happens, they are going to gain a little more strength, trying to accomplish this goal one more time. Your resistance is going to hold in this case and the price will then fall back to the support line that you have. This last phase is going to provide that second shoulder and will end this pattern. The containment line, which was the support during this whole process, is the neckline. An example of how this strategy is going to look in a chart is the following:

This pattern is hard to find because you may not be sure whether you are getting a double top or the head and shoulders, and you may miss out on some trades because you don't know what to expect. Most traders need to be in the market for some time before they can see this one working out. Treating it like the double top may be the best bet to help you earn a profit. But if you see that the "head" forms and goes way up and it has one shoulder ahead of it, you can get some relief knowing that there will be another raise on the second shoulder where you can make some profits as well.

The inverse head and shoulders

The normal head and shoulders candle pattern is there to help signal that there is a bullish exhaustion. If you then flip this pattern upside down, you will get the candlestick pattern that is known as the inverted head and shoulders. This is going to show more of a bearish exhaustion and it works similar to what we found in the head and shoulders, but we flip everything over.

After some strong bearish activity, the market is going to hit its support and then it will retrace and find the resistance. This activity is going to help create the first phase or your left shoulder. Just like with the regular head and shoulders option, it is hard to tell whether the inverted head and shoulders pattern is forming when you reach this first part.

After this happens, the bears will push the market down. This causes a false break, or a breakout trap, that is below the support that you already tested. When the price then shoots back up above the support, you will have the head section of this pattern form.

Next, the bulls are going to retest your support levels. At this point, the support will hold and the price is going to bounce back to the neckline of this pattern. This will end the pattern for inverted head and shoulders. The classic way that you can trade with this method is to just wait out the market and see when it pushes above this neckline. Then it is a good time to do a long trade. An example of how this is going to look when you see it on one of your graphs includes:

Squeeze Patterns

The next type of candlestick pattern that you may see is known as a squeeze pattern. Wedges are going to form any time that the market stalls because there is a period of indecision for that security. Then the market will start producing higher lows and lower highs on a consistent basis. This pattern is then going to compress itself into the tip of the wedge before the market ends up in a breakout pattern.

Once the price for that security reaches the tip of the wedge, there is a big chance that a breakout is going to occur. It is possible for a wedge to be bilateral. This means that the breakout you see could go in either direction. You need to have a good idea of the market and how that security has been doing to figure out whether you will see a breakout that goes up or down.

The classic method that you will use in order to trade these wedge breaks is to buy breakouts at the top of the wedge, and then sell it when the price breakdown below the wedge.

These are a few of the different candlestick strategies that you can use when you are working in the forex market. Many people like to use candlesticks because they can really help show how strong or weak a trend is and there are options of strategies that work no matter how the market is doing. If you are still looking for the strategy you want to use with forex trading, you may need to consider one of these candlestick methods because they are easy to use and great for beginners who are just getting into the market.

Chapter 10: Forex Trading Strategy 5 – Trading the Breakout

There are times when the market is going to sit in a range that goes between your resistance and support lines. This can be known as a consolidation. If you watch the chart, you will notice that a breakout may occur, a time when the price is going to move beyond the boundaries, either to a new high or to a low. Sometimes these can cause a new trend, and other times it is something that just happens temporarily. This means that the breakout could be seen as a signal that a new trend is beginning. Sometimes though, a breakout is simply just a strange pattern in the market and it doesn't mean you are going to get a brand new trend out of it. It is up to the trader to figure out when this is going to happen or not.

When in the forex market, these simple strategies need to be used with the help of risk management as well. This helps to minimize your losses if the trend goes the opposite direction than you predicted. A new high could indicate that an upward trend is going to happen with the security, and a new low could show that the security is about to go through a downward trend.

But how is a trader supposed to know what kind of trend is about to occur with the breakout? The amount of time that this takes will help you to figure out where the highest or lowest point will be. If you see that this new breakout stays away from the support lines for a very long time, it means that there is a longer trend coming, and the opposite is true with a short trend as well.

Let's take a look at how this strategy can go. We are going to take a look at how to work with a longer term breakout strategy. The buy signal is going to happen once the price finally has a new breakout that goes above its previous 20-day high. You can then look for the sell signal when the opposite occurs and you see the price goes below the previous 20 day low that you saw when researching. This is a simple method, which some investors like, but there is a negative to it. The main negative is that these newer highs may trick you into thinking there will be a new uptrend when one isn't going to happen. So, this can result in quite a few false signals in the market as well.

Working with a stop loss is a good idea because it can deal with this problem a little bit. To keep things simple, let's follow this basic rule when it comes to exiting the trade. Stick with a time-based approach. To make this work, you will close up the position that you hold after so many days pass. This may seem oversimplified, but it helps avoid the issue of the trade not working right when that trend ends up not going the way that you want. As a trader, you will want to exit the trade at a predetermined time and are set.

Remember that this one is supposed to be a long-term strategy. So, your time limit should be for at least a few months, or it is not going to work. If you find that these parameters are not providing you with enough signals, then you can adjust it to whatever you want. For example, you could make it a shorter term strategy and use hours rather than days.

Working with the breakout trend can be difficult for some beginners, even though it really does produce great profits if you are right with your predictions. You may want to take some time backtesting your strategies to see whether you would see results or if another strategy is the best one for you.

Chapter 11: Forex Trading Strategy 6 – Pop and Stop Trades

As a trader, there are going to be times when you are watching the market and the prices stay in a tight range. For this strategy, you want to wait for the trade to break out, which you will notice when it goes out of its normal range. The reason that you do this is that when the price breaks out of this tight range due to a violent move in one direction or another. If you can catch the trend at the right time, you can make money.

The issue with this option is that the price is often going to get away from us, even if we are watching it. This is because the price can burst through the range perimeter and then heads off like crazy. If this skyrockets, it could make a lot of money and the trader may feel that they missed a great move.

After seeing that big price change, you may want to trade with the breakout changes, rather than doing a chase price, with a lot of bad consequences when it comes to your money. Beginner traders will get into this type of trade after it has had time to start. They will then watch the move stall, and then that same trade is going to reverse, which causes a loss.

There is an urge to trade with that breakout. All traders want to be able to say they hit the ball out of the park on occasion. But for most traders, this is just not a viable way to make money, especially with the forex market. The strategy we are going to work with here is going to help those who want to trade on a breakout. It can also help you to build safety into the trade with the help of price action and the rejection bar candlestick pattern.

The image above is going to show how your price is going out of its range when the trading session starts. We may not have any way to know what made the price break upwards. Perhaps there was a new announcement in the news, or maybe a lot of big players in the market moved into long positions. No matter what caused it, the price ended up leaving its range and then, after doing this, it stopped for a bit. After the break, the price then kept going up. This is the reason this is known as the pop and stop trading strategy. The area we are going to focus on is indicated with the first white circle.

From here, we are going to see that there are two rejection bars that are bullish that form above and they will reject from the round number, which is our grey dotted line. Usually, when we see this kind of price burst out in either of the two directions, with a candle that is long and fast, it is reasonable for a trader to expect that there will be a retracement. This happens because that fast movement has covered an area where there are sparse orders, and these are shown on the chart as a gap in the market. These gaps are going to fill in at some point, usually sooner than later.

Now, there are a few reasons why we would want to enter the trade at this point. These include:

The time of day: For this one, the price may be

quiet before the trading session even starts. The start of the session is the time when we really expect the volatility and liquidity of the market to pick up.

The price was staying in a pretty tight range when it was traded. The price moved strongly in a fashion that looked like pop and stop. When you are doing this strategy, the pop of the price is going to go in either direction and the trader needs to be careful that they don't get on the wrong side of this or they could lose money. The price then forms a very strong rejection bar this will come with the round number. Ten another rejection bar will show up as well.

One method that you can choose for trading here would be to place the limit order about one or two pips that are near that rejection bar. You could have it right on the tails of your rejection bars for a trader who wants to be more aggressive with your trade. You can also take a more conservative approach to your trading here. To do that, you just place the stop loss just below the highs of your range.

With this second chart, we are taking a look at two possible trades that you can use with this method. The first one is known as the bullish rejection that will come from a round number. The polarity indicator will be that yellow stream that you can see in the chart and an old range, which will be hard to see from the left of the screen. The price had earlier popped above this range before forming another range that was based right above it. It works almost like one brick that goes on top of the next.

Looking at the second circle, you can see a candle that is very bullish. You can see that the first indication of a price stall because the wick that is on top of that candle is long. Then the second candle that we can see is a bearish one and it is going to complete what is known as a Harami Candlestick pattern. If you came in and traded long when you saw that first signal in the chart, this would then be a sign that you either need to take the profits that you get, exit out of that trade, or consider moving the stop up.

The final confirmation that you will get of a move that is going to happen in your rejection bar that is bearish. This rejection bar would have a very long wick that rejects from the highs.

This type of strategy is a very interesting strategy to use for those who want to take a shot at trading on a breakout. It can be challenging to recognize and work with, but it is definitely something that can result in a good profit if you can get in at the right time of the breakout, and if you make the right prediction about which way the breakout will go. With that being said, some of the things that you should be aware of when you want to use this trading strategy include:

Compared to some of the other strategies that you can choose, this one is kind of risky strategy. You are putting down money hoping that the gap that shows up in the markets sharp move will not be filled. You can also use rejection candlestick bars to help you confirm this move and keep some of the risks out of the trade. The pop and stop is going to work best when you follow the direction that other traders feel after they hear news about a company. So if the news makes traders uncomfortable about the company, you would want to trade in that downward direction. You should only use this strategy when the session is highly liquid. This ensures that there is enough support for that move to continue in its current direction. Make sure that you spend this time watching the news quickly. There could easily be a news announcement on the way that will reverse the sentiment and fill up that gap. Breakouts that work with this strategy will often show up when the forex market session first opens. This is because a lot of people will join at that time and it makes the market more volatile at that time. London and New York markets are good examples of this. You will find that looking for this pattern when those two markets open up can give you a lot of profits in a short amount of time.

Variations of this strategy can and do occur at the end of each session. This is not really a long-term strategy so you need to watch the market and make sure you watch for the changes that mean it's time to sell. This is also a scalping strategy. Always make sure that your stops are tight and then take the profits as quickly as possible. You can make a profit, but the trends can change quickly so you have to be ready to move quickly if you are using this option.

Chapter 12: Forex Trading Strategy 7 – The Moving Average Crossover

The next strategy that we are going to look at is the moving average crossover. This one is good for a beginner and is going to focus on the simple moving average. The SMA is a lagging indicator that will take a look at price data that is older, often older than what is found in most strategies, and it is going to move at a slower rate than what you see averages for the market price, The longer period that the trader watches the SMA, the slower it is going to move.

In many cases, we are going to rely on a longer SMA in conjunction with an SMA that is shorter. For this strategy, and to give an example of how this works, we are going to use a 25-day moving average as the shorter of the two SMA's, and then the longer one is going to be a 200-day moving average.

In the chart that we use above, the 25-day moving average is shown with the red line. You can see that in this case, it is going to follow the actual market price pretty closely, though there are some differences that you will notice. Then, the 200-day moving average is out dotted green line. Take a moment to notice how it is able to smooth out the price movement.

When your shorter, and also faster, SMA crosses the longer one, it shows that there is a change in the current trend. However, when the short SMA moves above the longer one, it means that the new prices are higher than they were in the past.

This example is going to suggest that there is a bullish trend right now. This means we see our buy signal. When the short SMA moves below the longer one, it suggests that a bearish trend is coming. This will be your sell signal. If this graph is right, and you are able to keep up with the trends and with the price movements in the market, this can be a great way to figure out when to purchase and when to sell.

Rather than just being used to help you generate the right signals for trading, the moving averages are going to be used as a confirmation of overall trends. This means that we are able to successfully combine these two separate strategies by using the confirmatory aspect of the SMA to help make the signals of a breakout more effective than before.

When we use this combined strategy, we can discard any breakout signals that don't really match the trend that we see overall by the moving averages. Let's look at an example of this. If we get a buy signal from the breakout we are using, we would then look at our graphs and see if the short

SMA is above the long one. If we see that it is, then we would place the trade. If this isn't true, then it is better to wait.

Chapter 13: Forex Trading Strategy 8 – Carry Trade

The final strategy we are going to look at is one that is used by professionals, so it may not be considered a beginner strategy, but it is still a good one to learn. The basics of this one are that you want to profit from the difference in yield that shows up between the two currencies.

The best way to look at this idea is with a little example. Imagine that a trader goes and borrows a sum of Japanese Yen. Because the interest rate in Japan is pretty low, the cost of holding onto this debt is barely anything. The trader is then able to exchange this yen into Canadian dollars, investing the proceeds into a government bond, which will yield about 0.6 percent. The interest received on this bond would exceed the cost that you had for financing that debt in Yen.

There are some negatives to doing this though. There is a risk that comes with this kind of trend. For example, if the Yen starts to appreciating against that Canadian dollar enough, then the trader is going to lose money on the trade.

These principles are also going to apply when you are doing forex trading and the same principles will apply. But there is going to be some convenience in doing all of this with one trade. You can then purchase a currency pair that has a base currency with enough interest rate compared to the quote currency, or the second currency, then the account is going to receive some funds from the swap rate.

The amount that you are able to earn is going to be related to the amount of currency that you command, so using leverage can actually be an aid that will work in this strategy. As we noted though there is some risk if you end up picking wrong with your currency pair. This means that any trader who wants to use this strategy, especially if they use leverage, needs to be careful when selecting the currencies they want to use. Inertia can be your best friend with this strategy and you ideally want to go with a forex trade that is not volatile. And if you do use leverage, remember that it can magnify your losses if you make the wrong decisions so be careful with that one.

With the carry trade strategy, you may want to work with the Japanese Yen if you can. This is a popular choice with this kind of trade because the rates found in Japan stay historically low, while still having a very stable currency.

You will find that the carry trade currency will work well during a time when there is a buoyant risk appetite because people during this time are going to seek out assets that are going to give them a higher yield. The action of traders who use this strategy can be enough to support the strategy. This works simply because the more people who decide to use this strategy, the more pressure there is going to be for that currency to be funded.

There is a problem that comes with this option though. In the global low-interest environment, the other traders are not going to have much of an interest in the differentials for narrowed interest rates. Then, when the appetite for risk has failed when we were in the credit crunch, there were many investors who got burnt as funds from this kind of investment flowed over to the Yen because it was seen as a safe haven. Since the Fed has signaled that it wants to tighten up its monetary policy in the near future, we may find that this kind of trade is going to come back into favor.

Some of the currency pairs that are popular for this

kind of strategy include EUR/ USD CAD/JPY GBP/PLN or even USD/RON.

Chapter 14: Forex Trading Strategy 9 – Fundamental Analysis vs. Technical Analysis

Some people decide to go with less of a strategy than with an analysis on how to pick the right currency types to work with. Many traders argue about whether it is better to go with a technical analysis or a fundamental analysis. Both of these are great options, so let's take a look at each one and see which one will work the best with your current trading style.

Fundamental Analysis

First, we are going to talk about the fundamental analysis. This option is going to involve an assessment of the economic well being of a chosen entity, or currency. It won't take into account the price movements as much. Rather, the trader would look at things like the GDP of a company, the debts it owes, and other things. A trader will use these data points to help determine how healthy the country will be and how long their currency will be strong. If the currency is strong and their GDP is doing well, then it is a good decision to invest in that currency.

When it comes to the foreign exchange, a fundamental analysis is different compared to what you would do for a company on the stock market. a fundamental forex trader is going to look at the whole economy of a country, checking the GDP, the trade balance, the inflation of a company, the growth in jobs for that company, and the interest rate that the central bank sets. By assessing the trend in these points, the trader is able to analyze how healthy the economy of the country is and whether they want to trade in that currency.

The fundamental analysis is not going to focus as much on the charts of how the company and its currency is doing. In fact, it is possible to do a good fundamental analysis and pick a good currency pair without looking at the charts at all. However, you will need to spend some time learning more about your chosen currency pair and their economies. This kind of analysis can take a lot longer to complete than just looking at some charts and graphs, but if you do a good job with it, it can open up a really profitable currency pair that you wouldn't have found with a technical analysis.

Everyday there will always be some news releases that will affect some currency somewhere. A website I like to visit for specific forex related news is :

Forex Factory

This website is invaluable for people who want to trade forex based on a fundamental analysis. Everyday that you are trading it is a good idea to begin by checking news releases that will affect the pairs you are trading with. You can set filters on this website to show news releases that will only affect the currency pairs you are concerned with. For instance at the time that I am writing this, the Spanish unemployment rate was just released. This statistic can affect people who trade the Euro as the number of unemployed people is an important metric of overall economic health.

One of the biggest monthly news releases that affects forex trading is the non farm employment change figure which is released at 8:30am New York time on the first Friday of every month. The non farm employment change figure is the actual change in employed people in the USA , excluding the farm industry. If you are going to trade forex based on a fundamental analysis definitely become familiar with this report! It has a major impact on USD currency pairs. Depending on the numbers released this report can move the market dozens of pips in seconds!

If the non farm employment change goes up, the USD value will go up against the currencies of other countries. This means traders can can buy the USD against other currencies or sell other currencies against the USD. You could buy long with USD/CHF or sell short with EUR/USD. If the opposite happens, if the non farm employment change goes down, the USD will go down. You can then sell short with USD/CHF or buy long with EUR/USD. This helps give you an idea of why it is so important to become familiar with the news if you are going to trade based on a fundamental analysis of the markets!

Technical Analysis

The technical analysis is going to be a bit different in forex trading. For an equity trader, they are going to analyze the price of volume on those shares that are traded on the exchange. If prices move higher with an increase in volume, traders will see that there is some demand for the shares of that company's stock and they will purchase. This kind of trader won't really look at the why of the price movement, but they will just look for the trends and see how it will go in the future before trading.

Forex is going to use some of the same technical tools that you would use in stock trading. A technical trader is going to assess the trend, the support and resistance levels, and the price action. Many of the patterns that are used in equities trading will be used in forex trading as well.

Those who use technical analysis are not going to use any secrets or "black magic" like some who use fundamental analysis claim. Getting started with this kind of analysis can be done simply by assessing both the strength and the direction of the trends. In fact, many of the other strategies that we discussed in this guidebook are based off a technical analysis. It involves looking at a lot of charts and graphs to figure out what currencies are the best ones to go with.

Both of this analysis can work well to help you pick out good currencies to work with. They just work in slightly different manners. Depending on the analysis that you choose to go with, you could use completely different currency pairs. And that is fine. As long as you use each one the proper way, you are going to see great results and some good profits in the process.

What are the Best Currency Pairs to Trade?

Everyone has their own favorite currency pair that they want to work with when they forex trade. The type that you choose will depend on your comfort level, how long you have been in the market, and what base currency you want to work with. For example, you could trade on the exotic market, on a market that is based off the United States Dollar, or other options. Some of the best currency pairs that you can work with include:

The Majors

The major pairs for currency are any pairs that go along with the USD. We will also include gold and silver in this list since these are popular to trade as well. Some of the best currency pairs to trade with the USD include:

EUR/USD: This is the Euro vs. the U.S. Dollar
GBP/USD: This is the British pound vs. the U.S. dollar

AUD/USD: This is the Australia dollar vs. the U.S. dollar NZD/USD: This is the New Zealand dollar vs the U.S. dollar USD/JPY: This is the U.S. dollar vs. the Japanese yen USD/CHF: This is the U.S. dollar vs the Swiss franc. USD/ CAD: The U.S. dollar against the Canadian dollar XAU/USD: This is for gold XAG/USD: This is for silver

The Crosses

You can also choose to work with the currency pairs that are known as the crosses. These are some good currency pairs that work well but are not going to be paired with the USD. The best cross currency pairs include:

AUD vs. CAD AUD vs. CHF AUD vs. JPY AUD vs. NZD CAD vs. JPY CHF vs. JPY EUR vs. AUD EUR vs. CAD EUR vs CHF EUR vs. GBP EUR vs. JPY EUR vs. NZD GBP vs. AUD GBP vs. CHF GBP vs. JPY NZD vs. JPY

The Exotics

There are also a few other pairs of currencies that can do well, but often they are reserved for those who are a little more experienced in the forex trading market. these ones are known as the exotics. These are the pairs that will go against a currency from a developing or an emerging economy. The other currency pairs that we talked about were for two countries that were developed and similar to each other. Some of the best exotics that you can try when entering forex trading include:

USD vs. TRY: This is for the U.S dollar vs. the Turkish lira EUR vs. TRY: This is the Euro vs. the Turkish lira USD vs. ZAR: This is the U.S. dollar vs. the South African Rand USD vs. MXN: This is the U.S. dollar vs. the Mexican peso USD vs. BRL: This is the U.S. dollar vs. the Brazilian real.

Many beginners are going to stay away from the exotic currency pairs. These exotics are not going to be as liquid as the crosses and the majors, which means there is a lot more risk in them. They can also be more prone to slippage, which means they are going to have a wider spread compared to the majors and the crosses.

Chapter 15: Common Mistakes to Avoid in Trading When Starting Out

All traders will have to learn how to manage the typical boobie-traps that often plague each of us at some point in our trading profession. In this chapter, I'm going to provide you with a list of mistakes that are common in trading when you first start out. Please do your research on each of these topics in-depth, and learn how to steer clear of them!

• Setting the wrong goals is deadly: choosing money as the only reason to trade is not a good way to enter trading. Chasing the money is what causes you to break rules and make mistakes.

• This is a business, not your hobby.

• Don't hold on to your trades that aren't winning. Let them go. It's okay!

• Don't start trading until you have a plan.

• Don't start trading without setting your stop/loss target.

• Go easy and slow. Do not start overtrading. This means you are trading too many different positions, or you are leaving positions open that leave you susceptible to market risk.

• Don't trade beyond your budget. This speaks for itself.

• Stay flexible at all times, and be ready to change your strategy to fit the current market trends.

• Stay up-to-date on news and events around the world.

• If you lose, don't let it affect how you trade next. Just step off for a minute, and come back with a renewed energy and plan.

• Set realistic expectations for yourself so that you aren't disappointed.

• Make sure you always do your pre-trade analysis.

• Don't go a day without writing in your journal.

• Do not jump around with different strategies. Learn one, and then move on to the next, after you have mastered the first one.

- Don't underestimate the difference between short and longer-term outcomes.

- Do not compare your profits to pips. The measurement of a pip has no value, but they are relative.

- Do not let anyone tell you that your win rate and your risk vs. reward calculations and ratios are of no use.

- Do not listen to anyone saying that you can make up to $2000 a day doing Forex trading. Look for platforms and brokers that speak in percentages. They are the most qualified and trustworthy.

- Do not blame technology and the tools you use for your lack of profit.

- Do not take price forecasts literally. It is nearly impossible for anyone to do that. We can only make forecasts and guesses.

- Do not trade to appease some thrill seeking journey you are on.

- Do not use negative words when talking about your trading life. Use positive reinforcements, and stay away from negative naysayers.

- Do not delay in getting a mentor.

- Do not watch how your account moves. It makes you emotional.

- Do not ignore the link between patterns and the market correlations. They are indicators of future trends to come.

- Do not risk the same percentage on each and every trade.

- Do not ignore the cost of doing business as a trader. Minimize your expenses as much as possible.

- Do not try to reel in a shark with a shoestring or a guppy with a fishing crane. Stick to what you can manage, and don't go too big nor too small.

- Do not forget the importance of statistics and math in your trades.

- Do not forget to create your trading checklist.

- Do not mess with your stop loss in the middle of a trade. Let it go.

- Do not expect to become rich overnight.

- Do not buy a robot to make trades for you. This is a big no-no!

- Do not get locked in on thinking a price will never change.

- Do not spend your own money if you make money during your demo phase.

- Do not forget to track, log, and analyze your performance on a daily basis.

- Do not simply follow uninformed advice from your uncle or your neighbor.

- Do not give up!

Chapter 16: Forex Trading Cheat Sheet/ Commonly Used Trading Terms

This is your quick reference guide—keep this handy. I've left some space for you to add your own cheats and tricks as you learn more on your own.

The Forex operates on a global timescale, twenty-four hours a day, seven days a week, with no start or end time. Given that no one stays awake 24 hours a day and that very little trading takes place on the weekend (from Friday at 13:00 PM US EST to Sunday at 17:00 PM US EST), the Forex trading day naturally breaks itself down into three major trading sessions:

1. Australia, New Zealand, and Tokyo marketplace 2. The London Marketplace 3. The New York Marketplace

These three marketplaces have currency pairings that each have their own individual characteristics that are critical to the "when" of trading.

Thursdays are the GBP/USD busiest day of the week. However, the other days of the week are also optimal for trading as well.

The best time to trade GBP/USD is anywhere during these time frames: 1:00 am - 1:00 pm EST

5:00 am - 9:00 am EST is the busiest time of the day to trade.

You can expect to gain anywhere from 90-127 of the total pips available in any given trend. It will depend on the day, however.

NEW:

NEW:

NEW:

NEW:

Commonly Used Trading Terms in Forex

From beginners getting familiar with the concept of investing to seasoned traders who have decades of experience, no matter where you are in your trading journey, it is imperative that each clearly knows the language used in the trading world in order to be able to make informed decisions, communicate, and analyze the data properly. For an extensive list of definitions and where these definitions have been derived from, refer to https://www.gdmfx.com/en/education/forex-dictionary [Forex Dictionary by GDMFX].

ADX (Average Directional Index) "A standard technical indicator that measures the strength of a trend."

Ask (Offer) "Price of the offer, the price you buy for."

ATR (Average True Range) "A standard technical indicator that measures the currency pair volatility."

Aussie "A Forex slang name for the Australian dollar."

Bank Rate "The percentage rate at which the central bank of a country lends money to the country's commercial banks."

Bid "Price of the demand, the price you sell for."

Broker "The market participating body which serves as the middleman between retail traders and larger commercial institutions."

Cable "A Forex traders slang word GBP/USD currency pair (Great Britain pound vs. US dollar)."

Carry Trade "In Forex, holding a position with a positive overnight interest return in hopes of gaining profits without closing the position in order to gain from the central bank's interest rates difference."

CCI (Commodity Channel Index) "A cyclical technical indicator that is often used to detect overbought/oversold states of the market."

CFD "A Contract for Difference — a special trading instrument that allows financial speculation on stocks, commodities, and other instruments without actually buying or selling those assets."

Commission "Broker commissions for operation handling."

CPI "Consumer Price Index — a statistical measure of inflation based upon changes of prices of a specified set of goods."

EA (Expert Advisor) or Robot "An automated script that is used by the trading platform software to manage positions and orders automatically without (or with little) manual control."

ECN Broker "A type of Forex brokerage firm that provides its clients direct access to other Forex market participants. ECN brokers do not discourage scalping, do not trade against the client, do not charge spread (low spread is defined by the current market rates), but instead charge a commission for every executed order."

ECB (European Central Bank) "The main regulatory body of the Eurozone's financial system."

Elliott Waves "A set of principles for chart analysis based on 5-wave and 3-wave patterns." Fed (Federal Reserve) "The main regulatory body of the United States of America financial system, whose division — FOMC (Federal Open Market Committee) — regulates, among other things, the federal interest rates."

Fibonacci Retracements "Levels with a high probability of trend break or bounce, calculated as the 23.6%, 32.8%, 50%, and 61.8% of the trend range."

Fibre "A Forex traders slang word EUR/USD currency pair (Europe vs. US dollar)."

Flat (Square) "Neutral state when all your positions are closed."

Floating Leverage "A leverage that changes depending on the total size of open positions."

Fundamental Analysis "The analysis based only on news, economic indicators, and global events."

Gap "A difference between the previous period's close price and the next period's open price. In Forex, usually only occurs during weekends — between the Friday's close and the Monday's open price."

GDP (Gross Domestic Product) "A measure of the national income and output for the country's economy; it is one of the most important fundamental indicators in Forex."

GTC (Good 'til Canceled) "An order to buy or sell a currency at a fixed rate or worse. The order is alive (good) until its execution or cancellation."

Hedging "Maintaining a market position, which secures the existing open positions in the opposite direction."

Jobber

"A slang word for a trader who is aimed toward fast but small and short-term profit from intraday trading. Jobber rarely leaves open positions overnight."

Kiwi "A Forex slang name for the New Zealand currency — the New Zealand dollar."

Leading Indicators "A composite index (year 2010 = 100%) often most important macroeconomic indicators that predict future (6-9 months) economic activity."

Limit Order "An order for a broker to buy a lot for fixed or lesser price or sell a lot for fixed or better price. Such a price is called a limit price."

Liquidity "A measure of markets that describes the relationship between the trading volume and the price change."

Long "A position which is in a Buy direction. In Forex, the primary currency when bought is long and another is short."

Loss "A loss from closing a long position at a lower rate than opening or from closing a short position with a higher rate than the opening. The loss may also occur if the profit from a position's closing was lower than the broker's commission on it."

Lot "A definite number of units or amount of money accepted for operations handling (usually, it is a multiple of 100)."

Margin "It is the money that the investor needs to keep at a broker's account to execute trades. Margin supplies the possible losses that may occur in margin trading."

Margin Account "An account that is used to hold an investor's deposited money for trading."

Margin Call "A broker's demand to deposit more margin money to the margin account when its size falls below a certain minimum."

Market Order "An order to buy or sell a lot at a current market rate."

Market Price "A current rate at which the currency is traded in the market."

Martingale "A position sizing strategy that involves doubling the bet after each loss."

Momentum "A measure of the currency's ability to move in a given direction." Moving Average (MA) "One of the most basic technical indicators. It shows the average rate calculated over a series of time periods. Exponential moving average (EMA), weighted moving average (WMA), adaptive moving average (AMA), etc. differ by the way of weighing rates and periods in the calculation."

Offer (Ask) "A rate of the offer — the rate you buy for."

Open Position (Trade) "A position on buying (long) or selling (short) of a currency pair."

Order "An order for a broker to buy or sell a currency at a certain rate."

Percentage Allocation Management Module (PAMM) "A broker-side system that allows investors to invest with traders and allows traders to manage investors' funds using the broker's platform."

Pivot Point "A primary support/resistance point calculated based on the previous trend's High, Low, and Close rates."

Pip (Point) "The last digit in a currency rate (e.g. for EUR/USD, 1 point = 0.0001)."

Profit (Gain) "A positive amount of money gained for closing the position."

Principal Value "The initially invested amount of money."

QE (Quantitative Easing) "This is a monetary policy employed by central banks. It involves buying and holding the financial assets from the country's financial institutions to provide money supply and keep the prices of those financial assets from falling."

Realized Profit/Loss "A gain or loss of an already-closed position."

Resistance "This is a price level where an uptrend stalls. Its breach can lead to a significant price rally."

RSI (Relative Strength Index) "A technical indicator that measures the power of a directional price movement by comparing the bullish and bearish portions of the trend." Scalping "A style of trading notably by a big number of positions that are opened for extremely small and short-term profits."

Settled (Closed) Position "A closed position for which all needed transactions have been made."

Slippage "This is the execution of an order at a rate different from expected (ordered). The main reasons for slippage are "fast" market, low liquidity, and poor execution quality by the broker."

Spread "A difference between Ask and Bid rates of a currency pair."

Standard Lot "100,000 units of the base currency of a currency pair you are buying or selling."

Stop-Limit Order "An order to sell or buy a lot at a certain rate or worse after it first reaches some opposite price level. It is a combination of a stop-order and a limit-order."

Stop-Loss Order "An order to close a position when the market reaches a certain rate. Normally, it is used to avoid extra losses when the market moves in the opposite direction. Sometimes, it can be used to lock in some amount of profit."

STP (Straight Through Processing) "A type of order processing that does not require any manual intervention and is fully automatic. In fact, 90% of all online Forex brokers support order handling with STP."

Support "This is a price level where a downtrend stalls. Its breach can lead to a significant price decline."

Swap "This is an overnight payment for holding a position in Forex. Since you are not physically receiving the currency nor delivering the currency you sell, the broker must pay or charge an interest rate difference between the pair's two currencies. Swaps can be negative or positive."

Take-Profit Order "This is an order to close a position when the market reaches a certain price. It is used to realize your profit."

Technical Analysis "An analysis method based only on the technical market data (rates, time, and volume) with the help of various technical indicators."

Trailing Stop-Loss "A stop-loss level that is moved closer to the current market rate as the position's loss decreases or its profit increases."

Trend "A market's direction established under an influence of various factors."

Unrealized (Floating) Profit/Loss "Profit/loss on your open positions."

Usable Margin (Free Margin) "Amount of money in a margin account that can be used for trading."

Used Margin "Amount of money in a margin account already used to hold open positions."

Volatility "A statistical measure of the number of

price changes for a given currency pair in a given period of time."

VPS (Virtual Private Server) "This is a virtual environment hosted on a dedicated server that can be used to run the programs independent on the user's PC. Forex traders use VPS to host trading platforms and run expert advisors without unexpected interruptions."

VSA (Volume Spread Analysis) "A chart analysis method that focuses on the trading volume and the price range."

Conclusion

Thank you for making it through to the end of Forex Trading for Beginners: How to Make a Profit Today! Let's hope it has been informative and able to provide you with all of the tools you need to achieve your goals whatever they may be.

The next step is to:

• Get Started and Pursue Your Dreams: Passion fuels focus, resilience, and perseverance. You need to have all three of these characteristics of a successful forex trader in order to pursue your dreams and your goals.

• Practice Makes Perfect: Research has shown that the human brain is functioning at its highest when it has had at least an hour and a half in one activity or another. That's why you see athletes and people who play musical instruments practice rigorously, every single day, and still maintain their rest. Relative to you as a new trader, this tells you that you need to allow yourself time to do other things. While this is a business, you don't want it to consume your life. Master the larger charts first. This also allows you to come back refreshed when we come back to it. The market is not going anywhere—trust me.

• Ask for Feedback, It's Okay: You want someone

who can break it down for you without being pompous and scholarly. That won't help you to make the necessary changes to your strategy. The most successful traders have identified what is working for them but are also constantly seeking the feedback of experts.

• Get Your Habits in Order: "The best way to ensure you'll take on difficult tasks is to ritualize them—build specific, inviolable times at which you do them so that over time, you do them without having to squander energy thinking about them." I personally, and many other experts as well, focus on prep before the marketplace officially opens or immediately after it closes. Remember my "surgeon philosophy?" They always prep before and do a post-surgery review as well. You have to get used to some hard work. Nothing worth having comes easy! We all know that.

• Document.Document.Document: You will realize the significance of having all of your progress in an organized journal as you gain more experience. You will essentially have a visual for your risk management and profit strategies right there for you. This helps you keep the mindset needed and we have talked about for Forex trading. This is the quickest way to success, by far.

● Get your demo account, and start trading. Don't be scared. You have everything you need to get started. It's go time! I know that once you put these strategies and practices in place, you will be on your way to earning a profit in no time!

"If you want to be really good at something, it's going to involve relentlessly pushing past your comfort zone, along with frustration, struggle, setbacks, and failures. That's true as long as you want to continue to improve, or even maintain a high level of excellence. The reward is that being really good at something you've earned through your own hard work can be immensely satisfying." ~ *Schwartz.*

Finally, if you have found this book useful in any way, a review on Audible or Amazon is always appreciated!

Stock Market Investing for Beginners:

Learn How to MAKE MONEY Investing in Stocks & Stock Trading! Become a Stock Market Genius! Investing 101 Everything You Need To Know!

account of facts and as such any inattention, use or misuse of the information in question by the reader will render any resulting actions solely under their purview. There are no scenarios in which the publisher or the original author of this work can be in any fashion deemed liable for any hardship or damages that may befall them after undertaking information described herein.

Additionally, the information in the following pages is intended only for informational purposes and should thus be thought of as universal. As befitting its nature, it is presented without assurance regarding its prolonged validity or interim quality. Trademarks that are mentioned are done without written consent and can in no way be considered an endorsement from the trademark holder.

Introduction

Congratulations on your purchase of Stock Market Investing for Beginners: Learn How to MAKE MONEY Investing in Stocks & Stock Trading! Become a Stock Market Genius! and thank you for doing so.

There is something very alluring about the stock market. Not only does it have historical significance to many people, but it also has been the secret to the financial success of many more. Even those with little to no knowledge of the market seem to understand the important role it plays.

Over the years, most have sat on the sidelines and watched as others have watched their fortunes made and lost within the blink of an eye. Everyone who has studied history knows that the Great Depression saw some of the worst financial conditions this nation has ever seen. Fortunes disappeared overnight as if they had gone up in smoke leaving many destitute.

We've witnessed the financial crashes over the last few decades and have heard of significant figureheads like Bernie Madoff (2009) who scammed more than a thousand investors out of $65 billion in a Ponzi scheme, or they remember when Enron went bankrupt taking many of their investors down the tube with them.

From the sidelines, you've likely watched countless investors lose their hard earned money, seen industry leaders hauled off to jail for fraud, watched lawsuits fill up the court dockets, new regulations implemented, and a host of other frightening events unfold right before your eyes.

In nearly every situation, the stock market was situated right at the heart of it all. It's no wonder that beginners hesitate to jump into the market and take a chance on this excitingly enticing investment strategy. Ask anyone new to the concept and they'll likely give you a litany of warnings; it's a scam, it's too risky, or you'll just be throwing your money away.

Yes, investing in the stock market can definitely be a risk but is the level of risk as high as many people believe? Is it really a closed market that is designed only to fleece the unsuspecting and reward those that already have so much? The answer to that question will depend largely on each individual and their approach to the market.

As the old saying goes, "Learn from other people's mistakes, you'll never live long enough to experience them all." As we observe the stock market debacles parade by, we can choose to use that knowledge to send us into a panic or as a stepping stone that will help us to avoid the many pitfalls that other people have fallen into.

The truth is that you don't have to give your money away in order to lose it. You just simply have to do nothing with it and you're bound to lose it anyway. While many people are quick to say that investing in the stock market is a gamble, without that knowledge and experience, they wouldn't be far from the truth, but what those people never fail to recognize is that everything in life is a gamble. We no longer live in a world where getting a well-paying job means security. We no longer live in a society that rewards hard work and dedication; a place where your bank will give you a reasonable rate of interest for using your money. That world, the one we have relied on for years no longer exists. Those who seek economic survival will quickly learn that they cannot always trust a financial advisor, they can't always rely on things staying the same no matter what, and they can no longer depend on a business staying in business year after year after year.

Our world is anything but dependable. The stock market, like anything else, is guided by simple rules. If you want to play the game and win, you must know these rules. That means you have to build up knowledge of the market and what you can realistically expect to receive from it. The more you know, the less risk you'll be exposed to.

This also means doing your homework like studying charts, reading reports, learning the patterns, and so on. Remember, knowledge is power. The more knowledge you have about the market, the easier it will be for you to make more profitable decisions.

But for the beginner, that can be quite undaunting. In fact, it could even be frightening to have to tackle these issues, especially if you have no background. In this book, we will endeavor to share with you information that will take away a great deal of the anxiety often associated with the market. We will walk you through the investment cycle step by step, teaching you...

How to prepare for investing in the market The fundamentals you need to know about the stock market Explain the differences between the different exchanges How to build a profitable portfolio Alternative stock investments you may not have considered How to value a stock How to analyze a stock And how to monitor a stock to make sure you're getting the best returns

We will even discuss key elements that will tell you when it is time to abandon a stock and move onto something that is more profitable. Don't get me wrong, it can still be a little scary, but it is not as hard as you might think. You can already dispel the myth that it takes a lot of money to make a fortune. Now, because of modern technology, you can start amassing your wealth with very little up-front capital, and you won't have to go into debt for it either.

There is so much information contained in the following pages that you'll probably want to read through it twice. You'll finish this book with simple, common sense guidelines along with step-by-step approaches to the topic that will give you the confidence you need to move forever forward on your road to wealth. So, if you're tired of working for your money, it's time to get your money to work for you. All you have to do is scroll down to get started. Right now.

There are plenty of books on this subject on the market, thanks again for choosing this one! Every effort was made to ensure it is full of as much useful information as possible, please enjoy!

Chapter 1: Fundamentals of the Stock Market

One of the most common misconceptions about the stock market is that it is all about the numbers. To the layperson, this just makes sense. Buy low – sell high, numbers are what you hear about. News reports tell us that the Dow Jones fell by 42 points today, NASDAQ finished at an all-time high, and the New York Stock Exchange reported heavy losses this week. If you're not very familiar with the market, you would assume that these reports are all discussing numbers, the Almighty Dollar, and percentages of profits, losses, earnings, and value.

Without the right knowledge, thinking in numbers is the logical conclusion. However, for those who work the market every day, they realize that the numbers are merely a reflection of something that is even more important. Human nature. A look deeper under the surface will reveal that all actions in the stock market give you a real internal glimpse at what is happening in the human psyche. It is crowd psychology at its best. So, while you are studying that endless parade of numbers before you every day, keep in mind that they are never what the market is really about.

As an investor, your goal is to try to determine what the majority of people will do when faced with very specific circumstances. If a company loses a contract, a plan for a merger falls through, or if a new invention appears on the scene that is in direct competition to a company you are invested in, what will the masses do?

Because the stock market is based on the age-old business fundamental of supply and demand, your best bet is to invest in areas where the demand will be high and the supply scarce. Your goal is to determine where the masses will want supply and get there before them.

While you may not be a numbers person, just learning this simple fact could be enough to make you take out those charts, study those squiggly lines, and analyze those numbers. They are there for a reason; to get you to understand the psychology of the millions of people who you will be throwing your hat into the market with.

Sure, everyone can lose in the stock market, but that doesn't mean you have to be a perpetual loser. The more you learn, the better your decisions will be and the lower your risk. Eventually, you will be able to amass a great deal of wealth, the kind that can give you real security and a steady income you can rely on.

What Does It All Mean? (Stock Market Lingo)

To do this though, you will need to learn the basics. No doubt, you've heard terms and lingo about the market that you don't fully understand. So, as you go through the pages of this book, you will find the definition of many useful terms in the glossary in the back. It will break down the new vocabulary we will be using as you start investing. Understanding these terms will be the key to help you avoid misunderstandings that could cost you a lot of money in the future.

Common Mistakes Novices Often Make

One of the biggest mistakes that novices make when entering the stock market is to not have a plan. Without an end-goal in mind, it is very easy for you to jump in at the whim of every advisor that says you can make money. While acquiring wealth through stock market investing is definitely possible, jumping in without a plan is tantamount to sailing a boat on the open ocean without a compass or a destination. You will eventually arrive someplace but without any direction, the waves and the wind will carry you to and fro at their whim. You, in essence, lose all control of your money.

There is no doubt that opportunities abound and all sorts of dreams can come true with the new stock market, especially in this modern day and age when even more exciting opportunities are being revealed. New companies are entering the market every day with new innovative industries, new companies, and new concepts being introduced. The world is changing and the old industries are starting to give way to new ones and when you're in on the stock market, you can be right at the forefront.

But you need a plan, a timeline, and a goal so that you can make your decisions carefully and in a way, that will put you on the right path. One of the first things you want to do is to find those advisors, columnists or other investors that are on a similar path with you and study their successes. Don't just listen to their words of advice, but study their track records. As you observe their decisions and the results they achieve, you'll be able to see how to create your own plan of action and pattern your movements in the market so they closely match theirs. You'll be able to identify patterns and formulate the reasons behind every move they make.

That, however, does not mean that you won't make mistakes. Even the most ardent of investors will misjudge conditions from time to time and end up losing money. It's important to understand that losing on a few trades here and there does not mean that you have lost or you have failed at stock market investing. It is simply an indicator that you are still growing. Still, there are some mistakes where a little knowledge can help you to avoid that. Below are just a few of the most common pitfalls that novice traders end up losing their shirt on.

• Buying stocks when they are extremely low: Many new investors start out viewing stock purchasing like shopping in the bargain basement. While on occasion, you can find an exceptional deal at low prices, most stocks that are extremely low-priced are usually there because of some negative obstacle the company must overcome. Stocks that are very low in price could be an indication that the company is facing financial troubles. If that is the case, it may not be possible for them to recover, and you could lose all of your money if they file for bankruptcy. It is better to buy stocks when the price is already on the rebound.

• Buying when the price is about to peak: It is easy to get excited when you see the price of a stock steadily rising, day after day or week after week. Beginners often follow the delusion that the price will continue to rise so they jump in without doing their due diligence. Usually, they've been sitting on the sidelines, watching the prices inch up higher and higher until they finally get the nerve to jump in. If they wait too long though, the price peaks soon after they enter the market and then begins a rapid and steady decline taking their investment with it.

• They hold on to falling stocks: There is a delicate balance between knowing when to HODL and when to let go. The hope is always that, if they hold on to a stock declining in price, it will recover. Unfortunately, that is not always the case. Anytime you see a stock suffering a significant loss of 7% or more, it is better to sell to protect your assets. If the stock does recover, you can always buy back in later on but at least your money will not be at risk as it continues to decline.

• They focus more attention on prices and dividends than on the company's history: The difference between a novice investor and a successful one is the research. Seasoned investors always have a plan and that plan is based on their familiarity with a company's history and the daily, weekly, and monthly charts. The more dedicated you are to researching a stock before dipping your toe in the water, the lower your level of risk and potential losses.

• They fail to set actionable goals and objectives: Without a target to aim at or a plan in place, investors tend to drift into dangerous waters. Deciding to build up enough for a child's education or enough to sustain you in your later years can be incentive enough for you to take care with every decision you make.

• Time Horizon is too short: If you're saving for retirement, keep in mind that life expectancies are much more advanced than they used to be. If you

have plans to leave some of your assets to others,
plan for a much

longer time horizon. Even if you plan to wait until 70 to enter into retirement, most people can reasonably expect to live an additional 15 to 20 years. When you make your plan, it is essential that your time horizon is placed far enough into the future for you to reach your goals.

• They pay too much attention to the media: Even when news events affect the stock market, by the time it reaches you, chances are it will have already affected the price of the stock. News media reports are often unpredictable. One analyst says this and another says something else. One says, don't buy, others say buy. To the new investor, it can be very confusing. Rather than spending your time following such contradictory reports, spend your time creating your investment plan and doing your research on each company you want to invest in.

• Failing to Rebalance: Rebalancing is the act of keeping the assets in your portfolio in balance so that you don't have too much invested in one particular sector. Many new investors are reluctant to do this because it may mean selling assets in a sector that is doing well and buying more of those assets that are not performing well. However, a portfolio that remains out of balance where some assets are overweighted in one area and underweighted in another area can set you up for some major losses in the future. Regular rebalancing can reap huge rewards in the long run.

• Too much trust in financial managers: There is no possible way to predict which financial managers will outperform or underperform with their investment strategies. Market timing is an art that is practiced over the long-term, and everyone will lose at some point in the stock market game. While it may be profitable to use a financial advisor to help you navigate this market, keep in mind that they are only human and have no real ability to predict the future. If you are using a financial manager, do not trust their decisions exclusively. You also need to be aware of market movements and the reasons behind their decisions.

• Chasing Performance: Most investors will select a particular asset class, follow set strategies and choose managers and funds based on a company's past history. This strategy has led to many more investment decisions than anything else on the market. Just because an asset has shown strong performance in the past is in no way a guarantee that they will continue to do so. Past history only tells you what you should have done in the past. While this information can play a role in deciding where to put your money, your investment plan should take in a wide variety of factors.

Most investors recognize that mistakes are unavoidable, but they take the time to do the necessary homework in order to create a strong plan. They are willing to make adjustments if part of their plan does not yield expected results, and carefully diversify so that they can protect themselves in a variety of ways. Remember, if you do your homework, create a plan, and then work the plan you are likely to be much more profitable than someone who believes too much, trusts too eagerly, and remains too loyal.

You will soon find that most profitable investment strategies that will earn you money are boring, to say the least. They are not those stocks that leap from penny stocks to hundred-dollar values in the course of a few months. They are those that inch up a penny or two at a time. These are likely to be the most profitable over time, and profits are the primary reason why we choose to invest.

Questions You Should Ask Before You Put Your Money Down

It may seem like a given that you would not put your money down without doing a little research beforehand, but you'd be surprised at how many get caught up in the excitement and toss their money in the pile and simply hoping for the best. If you know even a little about history, you will find that while this devil- may-care attitude may work for a while, it won't be long before the tables will turn; often with a sudden and very unpleasant ending to cope with. However, there is hope, even for the new investor, to make investing in the stock market a lot less painful.

The key here is to find a winning stock, so that means you need to know as much about the company as you can. While this doesn't guarantee that you will have a winning stock, it will make you a better-informed investor so you're less likely to take unnecessary risks. Below are a few questions every investor needs to know before deciding to buy any particular stock.

1. What does the company do? Never invest in anything that you don't understand. Make sure that the company you're considering is offering products or services that you can comprehend and relate to. If you are struggling to understand what they are trying to accomplish, then you have no way of measuring its success or whether or not its projections for the future are reasonable.

2. Is the company turning a profit? This question may not be so easy to answer. There are many variables involved in making a profit, but you can start to learn about them by reading the company's quarterly and annual reports to determine their net income and per-share earnings.

3. What is the company's earning history and future projections? A look at a company's quarterly and

annual statements over the past years can reveal a lot. It can show whether or not it has shown a steady earnings growth rate and if the stock has been too volatile over the years. You also want to get a feeling for if it is reasonable to expect a company's past growth to continue.

4. How is the stock valued? It can be exciting to watch a company's earnings continue to grow, but you also need to know how that stock is valued. You need to understand a company's price to earnings ratio (P/E) and price to sales.

5. What is their competition? All businesses have competition and their effect on the stock can have an equal impact on the prices you pay per share. Know how much of the market share your company owns and what are the competitors trying to do to steal it away. To that end, you also need to know the nature of the market itself. Is there one clear leader in their industry or is it divided up where no single company has cornered the market in their field?

6. Who's in charge? Find out who the senior managers are, their history with the company, their background, and their overall expertise. Do they have a stable management team or is there a constant changing of the guards?

7. What is the condition of the balance sheet? It is not enough to know what the company is raking in over time. It is just as important to understand how much debt the company is dealing with. The best

investors are fully capable of analyzing a company's balance sheet to determine the amount of debt the company owes. From studying the balance sheet, you can determine if there is too much-borrowed money in relation to its earnings.

8. What do the annual reports say? There are two kinds of annual reports you should look at. The 10-Q report and the 10-K reports detail the risk factors that could have a negative impact on the stock.

9. Can they sustain their present competitive position? Competition is a key element that all companies must contend with. Their present competitive stance may be proving effective at one point, but it is also important to know if they can maintain that stance for the long haul and if they cannot, what will happen to their earnings when they stop?

10.What is the company's reputation? Do they have above board accounting practices and are they honest enough to inform investors of depreciating rates on their assets? You want a good knowledge of their accounting practices and operating assumptions. From these, you can determine what the company believes to be its future growth rate and if they will take a more aggressive approach to growth in the coming years.

Of course, there are probably many more questions that will come to mind once you start your research. By carefully screening each company for these details, you start with a good foundation that will serve you well once you begin your investing.

Chapter 2: You and the Stock Market – Are You Ready?

It can be scary to invest in the stock market for the first time. While stocks can be an excellent long-term way of growing wealth, there are pitfalls that you must watch out for.

All of us have heard stories about large money-making corporations that started in a family garage and grew into a financial empire (MCST), and we all wish we had been there poised and ready to invest when the company first went public. But the reality is that the majority of stocks do not grow at such an impressive rate.

Before you make any decisions, you need to prepare yourself for what is to come. Right now, your financial portfolio may not be anywhere near what you hope it to be. While you may be a little naïve when you start, it doesn't mean that you are blindly walking along the edge of a cliff hoping that each step will take you in the right direction. There are practical things you can do to ensure that your stock market investing gets off on the right foot.

Structuring Your Investment Portfolio

In the world of investment, your portfolio is your most important path to success. You need to know your personal investment goals and where to allocate your assets in order to turn the greatest amount of profit. This involves taking in your own personal tolerance for risk and at the same time meet your future capital requirements for generating income. This does not have to be overly difficult but can be done by completing a few basic steps.

Determine the Best Asset Allocation to Meet Your Needs

One of the first things to do is to determine your present financial situation and your goals. This step will help you find your investment horizon (the length of time you are willing to use your portfolio to generate income for you). Young people generally have a longer investment horizon so are more willing to take risks since they will have more time to recover if they are faced with losses. Older people, however, tend to be more cautious and have a shorter investment horizon.

To determine your investment horizon, you first need to decide your end goal. It may not be possible to decide on an exact number, but you can determine how many years you plan to put into building your portfolio. A short horizon could be as little as one year or as much as ten and long-term horizons could be thirty or forty years. You don't need to come up with an exact number, but a rough estimate will be enough to start. This information will help you determine which investment strategies you will use.

You also need to know how much capital you will use to seed your portfolio. It takes money to make money so deciding how much you will use to start the ball rolling is crucial. If you have a hefty savings account set aside, this may not be a problem, but if you are starting from scratch, you'll have to make a few sacrifices. Some people have decided to forego the money they spend on a particular luxury or perk each week into the market. For example, if you have a habit of eating out once a week, you could consider only eating out once a month – using the money you save as capital to invest in the stock market. There was a time when you needed thousands of dollars to start investing in the stock market but now, even if you only have $1 or $5, there are places that will help you get started. We'll discuss those places later on in the book.

Your own personal financial situation and goals will help you get started building up your financial portfolio. You may also want to take into consideration your age and your level of risk. The more you understand about your personal needs and expectations, the easier it will be to determine what you will need to get your portfolio started. For example, if you are starting to invest in your 20s, then you'll have a lot more time to build up your portfolio and earn the amount of money you want. On the other hand, if you're starting in your 50s, your time horizon is going to be very short. In such a case, you'll probably want to be more cautious about your investment decisions because you don't have as much time to recover losses if something happens.

Build Your Portfolio: Now that you know what capital you have and your time horizon, you need to allocate those assets to build your portfolio. You can first break the stock market up into smaller pieces where you will place a portion of your capital in each one.

There are several areas you can divide them up into including:

Stocks Bonds Mutual Funds

Exchange-Traded Funds (ETFs)

As you develop your strategy, remember to carefully analyze not just the price of the stock but the quality and potential of it as well. We'll discuss more of this in chapter 4.

Assess your portfolio weights

At this point, you know how much you want to invest, how long you want to have this money working for you, and you have a pretty good idea of what percentage of your portfolio you want to put into each area. This is a good start, but to be an effective investor, you also need to look at your portfolio not just as a fixed plan but one that will need to be readjusted from time to time.

Because of the constant fluctuations of the market movements, the importance (or the weight) you give to each asset will change over time. Make a plan to review the asset weights periodically so that you're not blindsided by the various factors that could shift them and their effect on your investment plan. Once these things change (and they will), you will need to make adjustments accordingly. To do this, determine first which assets are overweighed (given too much importance) and which ones are underweighted (given too little importance), and then shift them accordingly by selling shares of those that are overweighed and buying more of those that are underweighted. Over the years, this will keep your portfolio in balance and offer an additional level of protection against risk.

How to Choose a Good Investment Broker

The steps above may feel a little too much

too fast for some investors. If you don't have the confidence in your ability to analyze and make those decisions, another option is to find an investment broker.

For new investors, you may feel like you are venturing into uncharted waters and would prefer the guidance and assistance from someone who knows the system to help you get started. Whether you choose to do this all on your own or not, an investment broker can be very instrumental in helping you learn how to find the information you need and ask the right questions so you can make a good decision.

Choosing the right broker should involve more than letting your fingers do the walking. Just because a broker has an ad doesn't necessarily mean he (or she) is the right fit for you. You will need to do a little research and give it a lot of thought in order to make the right decision.

It helps to know exactly what you can expect from your broker. There are two types for you to choose from: those who work directly with you (hands-on approach) and those who simply serve as intermediaries in assisting you with your stock purchases. The latter is often referred to as broker-resellers.

Within each of these groups, you can have a

full-service broker or a discount broker. Full-service
brokers offer more services but they come at a cost.

With a full-service broker, much of your research and legwork is done for you. They will give you one-on-one advice and even personalize their suggestions so they meet your specific goals.

Discount brokers do not offer much in terms of customer service. However, many will give you the option to get personalized advice on a specific trade if you need it. Because this is not part of their standard fee, you'll probably have to pay extra for that service if you choose to use it.

Choosing which broker to work with is entirely a personal matter. There are definitely pros and cons to each of them. When making this decision, however, there are a few things to keep in mind.

The Costs: Costs and fees can have a major impact on the returns you get. Many brokerage companies have minimum balances that you will need to open an investment account. These can range anywhere from $500 to $1000 to get you started. However, there are discount brokerage firms that require no minimum in order to open an account.

Margin: Margin accounts usually require an even higher minimum balance, but they allow you to buy stocks on credit so you don't have to put up a lot of up-front capital to rake in a huge windfall.

Keep in mind that with a margin account, you will have to pay interest on any amount you borrow in addition to the brokerage costs and fees.

Withdrawals: You also need to understand what their specific withdrawal fees are. These fees can vary based on their requirements. Some will allow you to make withdrawals only if your balance doesn't drop below a certain point. Others will provide you with a checking account but will come with their own fees associated with it.

When choosing your broker, make sure that you fully understand their fee structure. Do not open an account until you know exactly what you're going to get and what it's going to cost you.

Finally, find a broker that is willing to work with you based on how you want to trade. You need to know your personal investment approach BEFORE you choose a broker. If you're a trader, you'll want to make a lot of trades, jumping in and out of the market frequently. These usually earn money fast based on price volatility so choosing a broker with low or no trading fees will be important.

The other type of investor is the Buy and Hold strategy where they buy stocks and hold them for an extended period of time. These are usually more focused on waiting until the value of their stock appreciates and are happy to wait for their major earnings in the future. These will only make occasional trades and a broker's fee structure may not have a major impact on their plans. For this type of investor, you want to avoid any broker that charges regular monthly fees as they will most likely eat up any of your earnings you make.

Bottom line, regardless of whether you want to be an active trader, involved in every decision of your portfolio or if you want to be passive, you will have to have a brokerage account to buy stocks. Therefore, choosing the right broker for you will be the key to your investment strategy.

Stocks or Funds, Which is Better?

For the new investor, terms can be confusing. You hear things like stocks, bonds, funds, indexes, and a lot more. To the novice, it is difficult to tell the difference let alone decide which one is right for their plans. Even if you ask the experts, you will get different answers, each based on their own personal take on investing.

Basically, each has its own function so they will appeal to a different type of investor. To decide which one is best for you, there are four basic steps to take.

Step 1: The Savings Phase

Before you can invest any money, you have to have some money set aside to get started. You need to analyze which stage in your savings phase you are in. If you are just beginning, then mutual funds provide you with a setup that will allow you the ability to build up a savings balance. While most funds require a minimum of $1000 to get started, there are a few that will allow you to start with a smaller amount.

Mutual funds are easy investment options for the beginner because they have the diversification already built in. Stocks, on the other hand, are generally better managed by more experienced investors and allow you to tweak your portfolio and adjust your options in ways that mutual funds can never do. In most cases, stocks require a greater up-front investment capital with some accounts opening with minimums as much as $50,000 or more.

Step 2: Taxes

Next, consider your exposure to taxes. If you are looking for more control over how much your tax bill will be, then stocks may be your better option. They are quite efficient because gains are entirely under your control. Even if you choose to use a financial manager, you could find that their fees are completely deductible, so you could save on those additional costs as well.

If taxes are not a major concern for you, then you might opt to invest in mutual funds. However, it's important to note that their management fees are not allowable on your tax returns nor do you have the option to pick and choose when you will take your gains and will be exposed to capital gains taxes when you do.

Step 3: Your Investment Style

If you're the hands-on type of investor, then you'll more than likely want to go with the stocks. Mutual funds are often set to automatic with little to nothing on your part to do. It's a kind of set it up and then walk away for the duration. With mutual funds, you'll also find that you can't monitor the progress of the stocks and in most cases; you won't know what you're invested in.

If you're looking for something that is transparent, then mutual funds are not likely going to suit your needs. In such cases, a stock portfolio will be a wiser investment.

Step 4: Managed or Self-Managed

When your portfolio is managed, everything is done for you. You have professional investors at your disposal, ready to develop personalized investment strategies to meet your goals. You can simply decide when you want to get in the market and when to get out and everything else is done for you. These take into consideration a host of conditions like tax exposure, level of risk tolerance, your personalized investment strategy, and your income goals.

Mutual funds are much like the self-managed portfolio when you decide exactly when to get in and when to get out, but they can't be customized to meet your personal needs. Stocks, on the other hand, allow you to have more involvement in the decision but you may have trouble exiting the market at your target price as their trades are based on whether or not a particular stock is ready to sell and in demand.

Whether you choose mutual funds or stocks, there are definitely pros and cons for each. Your decision should be based on more than just the idea that they will do well. You'll each have to contemplate each of your decisions in order to get the best results.

How to Compare Companies

When you are ready to choose which company stocks to add to your portfolio, there are several factors to keep in mind.

Only buy from companies you understand: If you don't understand the business, you won't understand its potential. You may hear of a company that is on the cutting edge of something absolutely spectacular, but if you don't have an appreciation for this new invention or idea, then you're basically shooting yourself in the foot by putting your money in it. There are more than enough companies on the different exchanges that you won't have to put your money at risk with something you can't even wrap your head around.

What is the company's future: Do not focus entirely on earnings. This is not because earnings are unimportant, but they tend to cloud the judgment of new investors so that they ignore other more important aspects of the venture. To determine a company's growth potential, look at their statements, annual reports, and other data and compare the growth of revenue with the cash flow from operations. The growth rate compares the revenue stream for the current year with the revenue it generated in the previous year.

The company's cash flow: It is important to review their cash flow from operations, which can give you a clear picture of their sustainability.

Compare valuation: Valuing a stock is not very easy. One would think that if one company is growing faster than another that the faster-growing company's stock would be valued much higher. This is not often the case. The price of the stock has very little to do with the true value of the company. To truly value a company, you will need to use several tools:

a. The Price to Earnings ratio – P/E b. The Price to Free Cash Flow ratio – P/FCF c. The Price to earnings growth ratio - PEG

To find the P/E or the PEG, you can look on the company's website. However, the P/FCF can be calculated yourself by taking the total amount of cash the company earns from its operations and deducting the capital expenditures. Then take the market cap and divide it by the result and you get the P/FCF ratio.

Compounding

There is a lot more involved in building wealth than buying stocks and waiting for them to go up in price. People have been able to amass great fortunes this way. However, to really speed up the investment process, one must take it a step further. The concept of compounding your investment value makes it possible for you to accumulate huge sums of money in a very short amount of time.

For example, if you have purchased stocks that are consistently giving you a 5% return over the long-term, you can build up that money much faster by reinvesting your earnings as they come in. Imagine that you made an initial investment of $10,000. After the first year, you would have earned a clear $500 on that investment. Now, if in the second year you reinvested that $500 profit so that it also earns 5%, your return at the end of the year would now be $1,050 with a total investment value of $11,025. Do the same in the third year and each successive year and your wealth will begin to grow at an exponential rate.

This strategy will work no matter what your initial investment amount would be, so, if you only had $100, to begin with, then you could easily compound that into a small fortune. Even if you only had $10 to start with, the results would continue to grow at a much faster rate. The more of your earnings you continue to reinvest and the longer you keep the money in play, the better your results will be.

To add to this, look for those stocks that are

giving you a higher return as that will also boost the compounding effect even further. To further emphasize this point, consider the results you will get if you take your profits as they are earned rather than reinvest them.

Amount invested $100

Compounding the profits @5% Without compounding @ 5%

Year 1 $105 $105 Year 5 $128 $125 Year 10 $163 $150 Year 20 $265 $200 Year 30 $432 $250 Year 50 $1,147 $350

It is very clear that when you compound your results, there is a significant increase in total returns. By reinvesting the profits year after year, you could amass a great deal of wealth without having to put in too much effort.

Follow the Rules of the Game

There is a reason why so many people are drawn to the stock market. The lure of amassing great wealth is within reach. However, making money this way is also risky, so you need to follow the rules of the game. This requires you to exercise a great deal of patience and discipline. Getting too emotionally caught up in what might happen can cause you to make hasty decisions that will eventually destroy your portfolio.

This means making the time to do adequate research so that you understand the market and what influences it. There are no shortcuts. The stock market is extremely volatile, and the pendulum can flow both ways. You could amass a huge fortune or you could lose everything. To keep you in check, here are a few basic rules you can keep in mind. By following them, you can lower your risk and protect your assets while they are in play.

Don't follow the crowd. When your decisions are based on what others say and do, then you leave yourself open to losses. As world-renowned investor Warren Buffet recommends, "Be fearful when other people are greedy and be greedy when others are fearful." Always make decisions based on information, not rumor. Do your homework. Don't go by the name of a company or an industry. Choose businesses that you understand. Forget about market timing. While it is important to know what a good price is, trying to predict the top of the market or the bottom is not easy and few people have been able to do it consistently. Choose a price and enter and exit the market based on when the stock reaches that price. Always follow your strategy. Leave emotion out of it. Diversify your portfolio. Be realistic. Don't invest anything you can't afford to lose. Monitor your stocks so you can react accordingly.

If you are unable to follow any of these rules, then it may be a good idea to get someone to assist you. In reality, if you can't follow these basic guidelines, then there is a real good chance that stock market investing is not the right choice for you.

Chapter 3: What is an Exchange?

All stocks are bought and sold on a stock exchange. Basically, the stock market is where you go to buy or sell securities. In addition to stocks, you can also trade currencies, commodities, and futures.

There are different types of stock exchanges depending on the type of stocks being traded. You could find one with a physical trading floor like the New York Stock Exchange, where people are frantically screaming across the room, making hand gestures, and passing order slips for all sorts of trades back and forth. But today, most exchanges are not as chaotic. Today, trades are more often done with modern technology, so there is no need to yell and scream prices across a crowded room.

Probably, the most recognized stock exchanges in America are the New York Stock Exchange or the NASDAQ, but they are not the only ones. Many developed countries now have their own stock exchanges and with the right broker, you can invest in any one of these exchanges. The London Stock Exchange in the UK, the Toronto Stock Exchange in Canada, and the AEX in the Netherlands are just a few of the larger more active exchanges today, but there are many more.

The exchange a company will trade on depending on its market capitalization. When you take the total number of outstanding shares a company has and multiply it by the share price, you get the actual value of the company on the stock market. For example, if a company's shares are trading at $20 with a billion shares still outstanding, the company's market cap would be $20 billion. Not all companies will have market caps that high, but you will find many larger corporations like McDonald's, Apple, and Amazon can fit easily in this range.

On an exchange, companies will be ranked into three categories:

Large cap companies with market caps amounting to $10 billion or more Mid-cap companies with market caps ranging between $2 and $10 billion Small cap companies with market caps below $2 billion

There are two other smaller categories you may hear about, the nano-cap and the micro-cap, but these are not very common and would be traded in some of the smaller, lesser-known OTC or pink sheet exchanges.

It is important to understand that when you

trade on a stock exchange, you are not actually buying or selling from the exchange itself. It is merely a platform where brokers can buy and sell for their clients. The exchange's primary function is to provide a place where sellers can liquidate their shareholdings and buyers can acquire them.

The exchange also tracks all the orders for each stock to determine supply and demand, which sets the stock price at any given time. So, if you see a "bid price" for a stock, it is telling you that someone is willing to purchase it for that amount. The same is true for the "ask price," which lets you know that someone is willing to sell at that price. The difference between the two prices is referred to as the bid-ask spread.

The New York Stock Exchange (NYSE)

The NYSE is basically an auction-based platform where traders are physically active on the trading floor. Each trader, or specialist, trades only one specific stock, buying and selling in the auction. The NYSE is probably the most well-known exchange in America. A company listed on the NYSE has great credibility because it must meet very stringent requirements year after year in order to keep its position.

Those who trade on the NYSE also share some form of limited protection. First, any company listed must obtain shareholder approval before implementing any stock option plan or restricted stock plan. In addition, the majority of their board of directors must remain independent so that there is no bias when decisions are made.

The NASDAQ

The NASDAQ (National Association of Securities Dealers Automated Quotations) does not have a physical trading floor. It is the first all-electronic exchange that allows buyers and sellers to perform transactions on a computerized system without any need for a physical trade. All of its activities are done electronically where traders conduct all their transactions over the Internet. Dealers who trade on the NASDAQ have their own stock inventory and can actively trade at any time during regular market hours.

The NASDAQ has some of the same requirements as the NYSE. If a company is unable to meet these minimum standards, they are delisted (or removed) and dropped down to one of the lower exchanges.

AMEX

The AMEX or the American Stock Exchange was the third largest stock exchange in America at one time. It has since fallen into a more obscure role, where it once managed around 10% of all securities trades in the nation. Today, its role has now been taken over by the faster and more technologically advanced NASDAQ.

The AMEX is also known as the NYSE American. It was acquired by the NYSE Euronext in 2008. Most of the trading is with small-cap stocks, ETFs, and derivatives.

Minor Stock Exchanges

BSE – Boston Stock Exchange consists of the Boston Equities Exchange and the Boston Options Exchange. It was acquired by NASDAQ in 2007 CBOE – Chicago Board Options Exchange CBOT – Chicago Board of Trade CME – Chicago Mercantile Exchange CHX – Chicago Stock Exchange ISE – International Securities Exchange MS4X – Miami Stock Exchange NSX – National Stock Exchange PHLX – Philadelphia Stock Exchange

These exchanges do not usually trade the larger cap companies and may often present a higher level of risk. Many of the stocks traded may not be well- established or are unable to meet the higher demands of the larger exchanges. That being said, it does not mean that you won't be able to find some significant opportunities with them. Caution is definitely warranted in order to ensure the protection of your money.

Over-the-Counter Exchanges

Over-the-counter exchanges are those markets that are not traded on any of the above-listed markets. These exchanges concentrate on small companies or those that have been delisted from the larger exchanges.

Many investors refuse to even consider trading on an OTC exchange because of the higher risks associated with it. There are, however, some pretty strong contenders in these markets. Not all OTC companies have questionable or negative histories. Some companies prefer the OTC market simply because they do not want the added burden of meeting the requirements of the NYSE or the NASDAQ. That being said, it is important that you are extra careful when investing in these OTC exchanges, especially if you do not have the experience needed to pick a winner yet.

OTCBB – An electronic community of companies that have been delisted from the larger exchanges. Here, there are no minimum requirements for annual sales to meet.

OTC Pink – These are companies that are not registered with the SEC. Their level of liquidity is usually quite low and there are no requirements for them to submit any quarterly reports or 10Qs.

International Stock Exchanges

Foreign stock exchanges exist in many countries. They are the places that allow you to purchase shares of stocks in other countries. While nearly every country has some form of these exchanges, the most widely recognized are those in highly developed countries.

Tokyo Stock Exchange (TSE) – This is the third largest exchange in the world by market capitalization and the largest exchange in all of Asia. At the time of this writing, it listed 2,292 companies with a total market cap of nearly $4 trillion. Stocks found on the TSE can be large-cap companies (1,675), mid-sized (437), and what they refer to as Mothers (companies with high growth potential) (182).

London Stock Exchange (LSE) – Located in the United Kingdom, the exchange holds a market cap that is nearing the $4 trillion mark, making it the fourth largest exchange in the world and the largest exchange in all of Europe. It lists more than 3,000 companies with stocks from more than 70 different countries.

Shanghai Stock Exchange (SSE) – The SSE is the second largest exchange in Asia listing more than 860 companies and is the 5th largest in the world by market capitalization of nearly $3 trillion.

Hong Kong Stock Exchange – The third largest exchange in Asia, directly behind the TSE with a market cap of around $2.5 trillion and the fifth largest in the world.

You will find there are many other exchanges throughout the world including

BM&F Bovespa in Sao Paulo, Brazil ASX – the Australian Securities Exchange

Any public company must trade their shares on one of these exchanges. These are places that connect buyers and sellers, so they can execute a trade. Before you can begin to start investing in the stock market, it is necessary to determine your preferred asset class and find which exchanges offer you the opportunity to invest in the companies of that particular class.

While the two largest in the USA are the NYSE and the NASDAQ, these are not the only places where you can buy and sell stocks. With modern technology available to nearly everyone, it is quite possible for you to execute a trade with just about any country in the world with just a little bit of research to find the details.

Chapter 4: How to Value a Stock?

Trading on the stock market requires a bit of courage. With millions of shares of stock trading back and forth across the exchange, you'll soon learn that you have to be quick at getting a clear understanding of the ebbs and flows of the market if you have any hope of surviving.

One of the first things to know is that the exchange is more than just a platform where you can buy and sell at will. It is also the agent that tracks each stock's supply and demand and therefore, sets the price of each stock.

But buying and selling stocks is not as simple as going into the supermarket and picking your shares up off the shelf. You need to understand exactly what you're buying, how to see its value, and how to analyze it properly so that you know if you're getting a good deal or not.

What You Should Know About a Stock?

Most people understand that when you buy a stock, you are actually purchasing a percentage of the business, but that is as far as their understanding really goes. Many may also understand when they hear terms like the market is up or down that they are referring to the price, but for others, this may not be all that clear. So, let's go back to the basics and get a clearer understanding of what all of these phrases and terms actually mean.

Generally speaking, when you hear phrases like "the market is up" or "the market is down," these are not referring to individual stocks, but instead are referring to market indexes. A market index is a group of stocks from the same industry sector. An example of some familiar market indexes could be technology, retail, energy, or biotechnology.

Some of the most common indexes you've probably already heard are the Standard & Poor's 500, the NASDAQ composite, or the Dow Jones Industrial Average. These are often used as a tool to get a picture of the overall market conditions and can serve as a benchmark for investors to evaluate the condition of their own stock portfolios. If you are interested in investing in a particular index but don't have the time to research each company in a particular sector, you could actually invest in an index simply by purchasing a share in an index fund or an Exchange-Traded-Fund (ETF).

The Four Fundamentals of Stock Value

Like anything else, buying stocks is not as much about the price as it is about the value. Everyone knows that price and quality in any product is not always the same. So, how do we determine the value of a particular stock? Determining this is not always easy. However, learning the four fundamentals of stock value can make a huge difference when it comes to making a smart decision.

▪ The Price to Book Ratio (P/B)

One of the first things you want to look for when valuing a stock is its price-to-book ratio. This figure represents the value of the company if by chance it were to be sold and divided up today. It is sort of like the Kelly Blue Book for cars and can be a good indicator of what's really at the heart of any company. This book value does not just list the inventory and the earnings of the company but examines closely everything about it. This value will give you the total value of the buildings, property, equipment, and anything else that could be sold including the company's stocks and bonds.

The book value often fluctuates with the market because these companies usually have an extensive portfolio of assets that have individual values that often go up and down following market trends. This figure can also change depending on its assets. For example, companies in the industrial sector have value based more on physical assets that usually depreciate over the years.

Ideally, you're looking for a baseline to help you decide what the best price for a share of a company's stock is. If your goal is to discover companies with a high-growth potential that are selling their stock at low prices, then the P/B is the best way to find them.

Basically, the P/B is a value of a company's equity or its assets. The ratio gives you the actual market value over its equity; the difference between the book value of its assets and its liabilities.

To calculate this number the formula is:

Price-to-book ratio = stock price/ (total assets–liabilities)

So for example, let's say a company has $100 million in assets recorded on its balance sheet and $75 million listed as liabilities. The actual book value of the company would then be $25 million.

Once you have this figure, you can then look up the number of shares outstanding. If there are 10 million outstanding shares, each one would represent $2.50 of the book value (25 million). If the shares are being sold at $5/share, then the P/B ratio would come to 2 (5/2.50).

Why is this information important? The core of this fundamental is that the market is not always the most efficient in pricing stocks. Some stocks are traded at far below their actual value and others are traded much higher than their actual worth. By understanding the P/B ratio, you can look for those stocks that are actually undervalued so you can get in on the market before they reach their full price potential.

By using this strategy, you can find stocks that the overall market has neglected for one reason or another. If you discover a company that is trading below its book value, one of two different things is true: 1) the general consensus is that the asset value is overstated or 2) the company is not earning a positive return on its assets.

If the value is overstated, it may be a warning to avoid investing because there is the risk that the value will drop during the next market correction resulting in negative returns. However, if the stock is simply not getting positive returns, there is hope for new growth. Perhaps, new management or another change in the industry could turn things around boosting the returns. On the other hand, a company that carries a very high price per share in relation to its asset value is likely to give you a higher return on its assets.

It is important to understand, however, that the P/B is not a way to find a miracle stock. It is only practical when using it with capital-intensive businesses sectors like energy, transportation, or manufacturing. It does not measure the intangible assets of a company with a well-established brand name, its patents, or intellectual property. Therefore, it won't work well with companies like Microsoft where the lion's share of its assets lies in intellectual property and not physical property.

It also doesn't work well with companies that are carrying a high debt level or has undergone an extended period of losses. Debt can artificially push up the company's liabilities where they can literally negate all of the company's assets giving an unusually off balanced P/B value.

Other factors can also impact the P/B ratio, so do not rely entirely on this as your determining factor to buy or sell a share. Still, it offers a fairly simple to use measuring tool that will help you identify those companies that may have been undervalued.

- **The Price to Earnings Ratio (P/E)**

The second fundamental to use in finding a good stock to invest in is the Price-to-Earnings ratio. This is probably the most used of all the stock evaluating formulas. If you notice the price of a stock suddenly experience a dramatic jump in price, then the P/E ratio is at risk. It is possible to see a stock increase in value without providing significant earnings to the company, but it is the P/E ratio that determines if the stock can actually maintain that increase. If there are no earnings to support it, the stock price will eventually deflate back to a more realistic level.

Therefore, the P/E ratio can be used as an indicator of just how much time it will take to recoup your investment if the business does not see any significant change. For example, a stock may be trading at $20/ share and can have earnings of $2/share. It then has a P/E ratio of 10, which means that it will take you about 10 years to recoup your initial investment if nothing changes.

Basically, the P/E ratio is used to value a company by measuring the share price against its earnings per share. The formula for this is:

Market value per share/Earnings per share

What you're looking for with this formula is the dollar amount you could reasonably expect to invest in order to receive a single dollar of earnings.

In order to calculate the P/E ratio of a company, you must first determine what the earnings per share are (EPS). To find this number, you must look at the company's last four quarters, which can be calculated by subtracting the value of the share at the start of the 12-month period from the share value at the end. You will have to make adjustments for other variables like stock splits if they have had any.

P/E can also be extracted from estimates projecting value over the next 12 months. When you do this, it is referred to as a "forward P/E."

Another way to determine the P/E is to take the sum of the last two quarters and the estimates of the next two quarters and use those, but this method is less common and may not yield a reliable result.

Let's put this strategy into practice by calculating the P/E ratio for Wal-Mart Stores, Inc. As of the market close on November 14, 2017, the company's stock price closed at $91.09. Their profit for the previous fiscal year 2017 was $13.64 billion with a total of 3.1 billion outstanding shares.

This gives us an EPS of $4.40 ($13.64 billion/3.1 billion). $91.09/$4.40 gives us a P/E ratio of 20.70.

When you have a high P/E, it indicates that investors are looking for higher earnings in the future. Companies with a low P/E can be evidence that the stock is currently undervalued or that it is doing extremely well in comparison to its history. It can be very rare to find a company that posts neither earnings nor losses.

You can take this calculation a step further by taking the median value of P/E ratios over an extended period of several years to use as a benchmark to show if a stock is genuinely worth buying.

There are some challenges to using the P/E ratio to evaluate a stock.

1. When you compare P/E ratios of different companies, you should notice that the resulting valuations and growth rates of different sectors can vary. This is usually because companies in different sectors earn money in different ways. So, only use the P/E ratio when comparing companies in the same sector.

2. Always make sure that the data you input to calculate the P/E ratio is accurate. This is the only way you will be able to get reliable results. You should be able to find this information from a number of trustworthy sources. However, when it comes to finding earnings, the data may not be so

easy to find. Since most companies are solely responsible for reporting their earnings, this figure can be manipulated, which could possibly skew your results. Always verify your data through several reliable sources before you conclude that it is accurate.

▪ The PEG Ratio

Because of the limitations of the P/E ratio, you may need to take your evaluation a step further. Most investors take the Price-to-Earnings- Growth ratio or the PEG as well. When you use the PEG, you also take into consideration the earnings history of the company. This will allow you to compare the stock of one company with the stock of another company.

You can calculate the PEG by taking the P/E ratio and dividing it by the year-over-year growth rate of earnings. Ideally, you want to see a low-value result as it is an indication that you're getting better prospects for future earnings.

When you use the PEG to compare the stocks of different companies, you will be able to see how much growth you can anticipate. A

PEG of 1 indicates the break-even point, a PEG of 2 shows you're paying twice as much as a PEG of 1.

Keep in mind that the P/E ratio will only give you a glimpse of a company's current financial condition, but the PEG gives you a graph that shows its history. As an investor, it is up to you to determine based on the data before you if it is reasonable to expect the future to continue in the same direction.

This is why a low P/E ratio is not always an indication that a particular stock is a good buy. But when you take into consideration its growth rate, you can end up with an entirely different story. The lower the PEG, the more likely that the stock has been undervalued.

There are several ways to calculate the PEG ratio but before you can do that, you will have to calculate the P/E ratio (explained above).

Once the P/E ratio is determined, the formula is:

PEG ratio = P/E ratio earnings growth rate.

Let's look at an example:

Company A has a per share price of $46. It has an EPS of $2.09 for the current year. It has an EPS of $1.74 for the previous year.

Company B has a per share price of $80. It has an

EPS of $2.67 for the current year. It has an EPS of $1.78 for the previous year.

Now, you have to calculate for each company:

Company A has a P/E ratio = $46/$2.09 = 22
Earnings growth rate = ($2.09 / $1.74) – 1 = 20%
PEG ratio = 22/20 = 1.1

Company B has a P/E ratio = $80 / $2.67 = 30
Earnings growth rate = ($2.67 / $1.78) – 1 = 50%
PEG ratio = 30 / 50 = 0.6

At first glance, Company A may appear to be the better deal. It has a lower P/E than Company B. But when you have all the data before you, it is clear to see that it doesn't have a sufficient growth rate to support its P/ E. You can conclude that Company B is the better bargain as you will be paying less for each unit of earnings growth.

▪ Dividend Yield

The fourth fundamental you need to learn is how to calculate the dividend yield. This figure is a financial ratio that shows just how much a company is paying in dividends each year in relation to the price of its shares. When you research the stock, you will see the dividend yield shown as a percentage. It can be calculated by taking the dollar value of the dividends paid in a given year by the dollar value of a single share of stock.

The formula looks like this:

Annual Dividends paid per share Price per share

Why is this fundamental concept so useful? It gives you a means of measuring just how much cash flow an investor receives for every dollar they invest. It is basically a way of calculating how much return on your investment you will pay for a particular stock.

For example. A company is trading its stock for $20/share, and it is paying an annual dividend of $1/share. Another company is trading its stock at $40/share but offers the same $1/share in dividends. The first company's dividend yield would be 5% (1/20 = 0.05) and the other company's dividend yield would be 2.5% (1/40 = 0.025%).

If you consider every other factor as equal,

then as an investor, you would likely choose the first company as the better deal. It gives you double the dividend yield.

This tool is very useful if you are the type of investor looking to build up a steady flow of cash from your investment portfolio. Dividend investing is very popular among popular value investors such as Warren Buffett. Companies that pay high dividends may cost you in other ways though. Every dollar a company has to pay out in dividends is money that they are not reinvesting in the company. So, even though you are paid for holding onto your stocks, it is possible that you will earn even higher returns without the dividends.

It is also important to understand that if a company is paying higher than usual dividends, it can tell you a lot about its stock. It may be undervalued or it is working extra hard to attract new investors. But if a company is paying little to no dividends, it could mean that it is reinvesting its returns in order to grow capital.

If you plan on being a dividend investor, this type of information can be very useful, but you need to exercise caution when you use it. Just because a company offers high dividends to its shareholders is not a guarantee that they will continue to do so. There have been many cases where a company has had to cut its dividends or even eliminate them altogether in order to ensure their financial solvency.

You can evaluate a company's dividend history and use it to estimate what their future dividend payments will be. This can be done by taking the most recent dividend and multiplying it by 4 if they pay their dividends quarterly. If they pay monthly, you would multiply by 12. While rare, some companies only pay semi-annually or annually. The result you get is referred to as the "forward dividend yield," and gives a fairly reliable estimate of what the future payments may be.

How to Analyze a Stock

A good stock analysis is a key factor in investing success. It is the most reliable means of finding those gems of a stock that can produce potentially profitable returns. The fundamentals we just went through can be considered different forms of technical analysis. These allow you to get a closer look at the supply and demands of any stock within the market. Investors who rely on this form of analysis rely heavily on a stock's historical performance and use it as a predictor of what they could reasonably expect in the future. With technical analysis, there is a great deal of emphasis on trends, charts, and patterns.

There is, however, another method of analyzing stocks that is very different from performing a technical analysis. Fundamental analysis is a very broad area that can be difficult for newbies to the market to master. It requires the investor to be familiar with a number of different variables including financial statements, regulatory findings, and a number of different valuation techniques.

While we won't be able to cover all the elements of fundamental analysis in the following pages, the information that follows should be sufficient to give you a basic understanding of what it is and how it works. As a new investor, this information is the key to your success in the stock market. It should lay for you a solid foundation of the concepts and how to use them to make wise choices in which stocks to pick.

A core element in fundamental analysis is studying a company's financial statements. This is sometimes referred to as performing a quantitative analysis. You will be looking at its assets, expenses, liabilities, and its overall revenue as well as many other aspects of the company. The goal is to develop a better picture of its future.

At its most elementary level, it is a technique that will determine the true value of a stock by concentrating your interest on the very factors that could have a direct impact on a company's business and its future potential. You do not have to limit your fundamental analysis to a particular stock. You can apply the same techniques to industries as well.

The goal of this type of analysis is to answer some very specific questions:

1. Is the company's revenue stream growing or declining? 2. Is the company able to turn a profit? 3. Is the company's position strong enough to beat the competition? 4. Can the company pay its debts? 5. Is management bookkeeping above board?

These are not the only questions you might have, but they are enough for you to get the general idea of the goal of fundamental analysis. Bottom line, you want to know if their stock is worthy of your investment.

The Fundamentals of Fundamental Analysis

Basically, you are looking at the fundamentals of the business; those things that make up its foundation. This can involve anything related to the financial health of the company. At the very least, it should include a close inspection of revenue and profit, but it can go much further and deeper than that and involve anything from the price of a share to how the business is managed.

These fundamentals can be divided up into two different categories:

▪ Quantitative: factors that can be measured in numerical terms

▪ Qualitative: factors that are related to quality.

Neither of the two is better than the other. They each have their own set of pros and cons. Qualitative factors are often associated with hard facts whereas quantitative factors tend to be more abstract. As an example, a company's quantitative factors could be its dividends, earnings per share, P/E ratio and other things that can be physically determined, but its brand recognition, its public image, and its value to the community would be considered its qualitative factors. No analyst would consider one without taking the time to look carefully at the other.

You also have to factor in other things like the company's intrinsic value. One of the primary assumptions when doing this type of analysis is that the price of a single share of stock rarely reflects its true value. If that were the case, doing a price analysis wouldn't be necessary. You're doing this to find the intrinsic value of a stock looking for any that are trading at prices below that value.

Another basic truth about the stock market is that over time, the fundamentals will always reveal themselves. We may not know exactly when that will happen but eventually, the market will correct itself and the true value of the stock will be reflected in the market price. Hopefully, you will be able to get in before that inevitable time comes, no matter how long it takes.

As you start your fundamental analysis, you need to look at the qualitative aspects of the company. These represent elements that are often complex and difficult to give a real value to. However, learning how to incorporate all that information into your research can help you form a solid conclusion as to its impact on the intrinsic value of the company.

The Business Model: Understanding what the company does can give you a good overall picture of its stock potential. You need to understand exactly how the company makes money. If you're dealing with a well-known company like Coca-Cola or Starbucks, then this is an easy step, but if you're looking at a company that may not be so familiar to the public, you can quickly find out this information by visiting their website and looking at their 10-K filing.

Still, even if you are researching a well-known company, don't assume that you know how its revenue is generated. There are companies that give a public impression of one thing but do something entirely different behind closed doors.

Boston Chicken for example; once thought

of as one of the fastest growing and most popular fast food chains in America. On the surface, one would assume that their primary business was selling chicken and that was where their profits were coming from. But it soon became apparent that their money was generated almost entirely from their expensive franchise fees. When it was later revealed that the franchises were continuously losing money, the whole business collapsed and fell into bankruptcy.

This is why understanding the business model of the company can be invaluable. If you were only doing a technical analysis, you would follow the numbers and they would give the impression that it was a profitable company and while the history was not a guarantee of future performance, you would have developed a false sense of confidence that it would continue in that same vein. Until you understand how a business works and generates its revenue, you would always be putting your money at a higher risk and leave yourself unprotected if something should happen.

Competitive Advantage: Another qualitative analysis that is a key to a fundamental analysis is the competitive advantage a company has. Its key to success is their ability to stay ahead of the competition and hold their position. An indication of a competitive advantage could come in many forms including name recognition in companies like Amazon and Apple. These companies are more than capable of positioning themselves miles ahead of their competitors and it would take major moves for any trailing businesses to catch up, let alone surpass them. As a result, shareholders can reap the benefits of higher earnings that could last for many years.

Some of the key elements of competitive advantage are:

- A strong competitive position

- Activities that are geared to the company's strategy

- A system that ensures sustainability

- Operational effectiveness

Management: Every company needs good leadership in order to stay strong. This is the key element that will steer the company in the right direction. No matter how good the business model is, if there is poor management, then its chances of success are limited at best.

But how do you gauge the quality of a COO or a CEO of a company? If you're not a professional investor, then you will need to know some basic elements to look for. You can't meet one-on-one with them, so you need to be able to find information that you can access easily online or from their published materials.

First, you should visit their website. Every public company is required to offer an information page on their site, which includes a short bio for each executive in the company. There, you will find their employment history, educational background, and past achievements. On this page, you will find a great deal of positive information about their leadership, but what you won't find is any negative information about their background. However, to get a more balanced picture of management, there are a few other places you can look.

- The CEO, CFO, and COO should be holding at least quarterly conference calls. Listen to those calls to see what you can learn. Initially, the beginning of each call is going to detail the company's financial results, which is information you can pretty much find on their website. You want to focus in on the question and answer portion in the second half of the call when financial analysts are free to ask direct questions to the management. Their answers can say quite a bit. Are they open and forthright or are they evasive in their answers?

- You can also look at their annual report. The Management Discussion and Analysis at the beginning of the report will give you a clear picture of the management's overall outlook for the company. It would be a good idea to compare this information with past annual reports to see if there has been some type of shift in vision and why.

- Nearly every large corporation will compensate their upper-level executives with bonuses, stocks, or options. If this is happening, it is a good sign that those who are in management positions are also

shareholders in the company. When that is the case,
you can be sure that

they are looking out to make sure that their interests (and by extension) your interests are protected. It can be comforting to know that the majority of the management team has a vested interest in the stock, so you can be sure that the decisions they make are less likely to have a negative impact on their returns.

▪ It can also pay to take a close look at the past performance of the executive team. How well did they steer the ship when they were at other companies in the past? Look at their bios and identify the companies they worked for and do a little digging to see how well they performed. It can be very informative to learn why they moved from one company to the next and what the condition of the former company was after they left.

Corporate Governance: A close look at the company's organizational policies and the relationship that exists between management and stakeholders. These will give you a good idea of the company's internal character and if they are complying with governmental regulations. Understanding their by-laws and regulations can help to reveal the types of checks and balances that are in place and how easy it would be for unethical practices to happen.

Ideally, look for transparency. It is not enough that they file their papers on time, but they must also disclose information about how operations are conducted. Transparency also means that their financial releases will be written in a manner that even non-financial experts can understand and follow.

Find out to what extent the company is willing to go to protect the rights of their stakeholders. As partial owners of the business, they should have some access to the management team or a means of expressing their concerns. What are shareholders voting rights and how can they be exercised?

Examine closely the Board of Directors, which should consist of representatives from both inside and outside of the company. This should create a balance of independent assessment of how the management team is performing.

As you look at the Board, look for some level of independence. Their role is to protect the shareholder and ensure that management is looking out for them as well. For that reason, there should be some level of independence that works separately from management so that they are free to fire and hire members on behalf of the shareholders whenever needed.

Each industry differs in some way from the others. They may have a different customer base, market share, rate of growth, competition, or business cycle. You need to also look carefully at these elements to help get a better understanding of the company's financial health.

Customers: Look for the size of their customer base. If a business is dependent on a very small customer base, the loss of even a single customer could be catastrophic.

Market Share: A company's share of the business can tell a great deal about their rate of success. If their market share is a mere 5% of the business, it can tell an entirely different story than if they hold an 80%. One company is not able to overtake the competition, but the other is leaps and bounds ahead of it.

Industry Growth: A look at the industry can also reveal much about a company. If the industry overall is expected to grow their customer base, then there are many possibilities for the future. A zero or negative prospective growth rate would be cause for concern. A company that produced cellphones thirty years ago would have been soaring in business but today, with the advent of smartphones and other technologies, they would be struggling to stay afloat. Look to see what the industry is doing for the future and what the company is doing to keep up with it.

Competition: Examine the competition the company is up against. Also, look at the overall view of the industry. If it has a lot of competition, there may be other problems that may be addressed;

supplier favoritism towards larger companies, the ability to pass on costs to customers may be limited, marketing costs, etc.

Regulation: How much regulation is the company under? Some industries are very heavily regulated by the government, which could have an impact on the company's ability to grow. For example, utility companies don't usually have a lot of competition; they are often up against only one or two competitors at best, but they are heavily regulated, which could limit just how much profit the company can realistically expect.

How to Read a Financial Statement

Reading financial statements can be overwhelming and confusing for the new investor. The sheer number of numbers can be unnerving. But if you learn a few little tricks to help you understand them, they can provide a wealth of information.

Financial statements are the primary means by which a company reveals its financial condition and is the tool most often used to make investment decisions. There are three types of financial statements you should be concerned with: Balance Sheets, Cash Flow Statements, and Income Statements.

Balance Sheets: The Balance sheet is a record of all of a company's financial matters in one statement. It records the assets, equity, and liabilities for a specified point in time. Its purpose is to bring balance to the business' financial structure with the following formula:

Liabilities + Shareholders/Equity = Company Assets

Assets are the resources that the business owns or controls: buildings, cash, inventory, equipment, etc.

Liabilities + Shareholders/Equity is the total value of resources the company uses to acquire the above assets. This could include financing costs, debt, and equity, etc.

The Balance Sheet gives a clear view of the financial health of the company. You can learn how much the company owns, what it owes, and its overall equity. When analyzing the Balance Sheet, there are three main areas you want to focus on.

1. Assets: There are two different types of assets to review. Current assets are those used during a single business cycle (a fiscal year, for example) and consist of any cash on hand, inventory, and account receivables. Non- current assets could be anything that is not included in the current asset column. Inventory can be any finished product that has yet to be sold, which could be a concern if the business has a large amount of inventory that is not moving.

Receivables are any uncollected bills still outstanding.

Non-current assets are anything that is not considered a current asset. This could be anything from a property, equipment, or any other type of fixed asset. In most cases, there is little need to focus on non- current assets unless the business is in trouble and is looking to liquidate.

2. Liabilities: There are two kinds of liabilities, current and non-current. Current liabilities are those that must be settled within a year such as paying suppliers, contract obligations, etc. Non-current liabilities are those that the company will take a longer period of time to pay off like bank debt or bonds.

You want to see a company with a reasonable amount of debt. It is good to see debt levels dropping and more assets than liabilities. If they are buried in debt that far exceeds their assets, you need to look a little closer to find out why. It may be the first signs that there is bankruptcy at some point in their future. To determine the asset to liability ratio, use the following formula:

Current assets – inventory

Current Liabilities

3. Equity: the amount of equity is the percentage of the company owned by the shareholders. It is the result of the above formula, total assets less the total amount of liabilities.

This information can be found in two places. 1) Paid-in Capital and 2) retained earnings. Paid-in-capital is the money shareholders paid for their share of the stock when it was first offered publicly and shows just how much money the company received for the sale of its shares. Retained earnings, however, is a listing of the money the company has used to reinvest in the business rather than distribute out to the shareholders.

Income Statement: The Income Statement gives you a clear picture of how well the company has been performing over a set period of time. It details the revenues, expenses, and the profit generated as a direct result of the operations performed.

Probably the first statement you will look at is the income statement, which is usually contained within the annual or quarterly report. When it comes to analyzing this document, you will look for anything that tells you how well the business is doing. You should be able to see that the business is making money by bringing in more revenue than they are spending.

Look for those companies that have low expenditures and higher returns in revenues. These are strong fundamental indicators that are priceless to investors. Revenue or sales are probably the easiest parts of the statement to find. There should be a single number that explains exactly how much money the company brought in. If a company is working to improve their profitability, you should see an increase in sales revenue. The best revenues you can see are those that continue to increase year after year.

Expenses can look different from one statement to another. The most common terms you'll find are the Cost of Goods Sold (COGS) and the Selling, General, and Administrative Expenses (SG&A). The COGS is the amount of money the company paid out in order to generate new revenue and the SG&A figure will include any money spent on marketing, salaries, or overhead bills to keep the business operational.

The Income Statement should also include the formula:

Revenue – Expenses = Profits

Basically, profit is what's left over after you have paid all of your bills. But on a financial statement, there may be a number of subcategories that will tell you how well the company is really doing.

• Gross profit is revenue less the cost of sales

• Operating profit is revenues less the cost of sales and SG&A

• Net income is the company's profit after they have paid all of their expenses. It is the bottom line and the kind of profit that most investors are looking for; the company earnings.

If the company has a high profit, it is usually evidence that they are managing their competition well. When they have a higher net profit, they have a level of protection in case they meet up with hard times later on.

Statement of Cash Flows: This records the amount of cash that flows in and out of the business over a specified period of time. It should detail the following activities:

• Operating Cash Flow: any cash resulting from everyday operations

• Cash from Investing: Any cash the company used to invest in acquiring new assets, proceeds from the sale of other owned businesses, equipment, or other assets.

▪ Cash from Financing: Any cash paid out or received in relation to borrowed funds.

While other financial records could be manipulated or skewed by the company, it is very difficult for anyone to manipulate the cash flow statements. For this reason, the cash flow statement is considered one of the most reliable documents a company can release.

It is different from the Income Statement in how the data is accounted. With accrual accounting, the method used to create an Income Statement, transactions are recorded when they occur and not when they are exchanged. This can make a huge difference in the bottom line.

If the income statement shows a net income of $100, it does not necessarily mean that the cash is in hand even though the balance is increased by $100. However, when the same $100 is included in the Statement of Cash Flows, that's exactly what it means. It is indicating a "true" cash profit; a critical component of doing a fundamental analysis.

The Cash Flow Statement has three sections:

• Cash Flows from Operating Activities: how much cash is coming in from the sale of goods and services, less the cash necessary to make and supply those goods. Ideally, you want to see a net positive cash flow in this area.

• Cash Flows from Investing Activities: the amount of cash the company spends on its expenditures to keep the business running. This could include new equipment needed, acquisitions, or investments. You're looking for a company that is actively re-investing capital in its business at a rate that is equal to or greater than the rate of depreciation each year. If there is no reinvestment plan, the cash flows could be artificially high and may not be sustainable.

• Cash Flow from Financing Activities: includes any cash used in relation to outside financing. Money is raised from selling financial holdings like stocks and bonds. It should also show the outflow of cash used to pay down a bank loan or dividend payments.

When it comes to Cash Flow Statements, you are looking for companies that show they can generate lots of free cash flow. This is a sign that the company is strong enough to pay their debts, dividends, and other financial obligations and still grow their business. The formula for calculating

Free Cash Flow is as follows:

Net Income + Amortization/Depreciation

- Changes in Working Capital - Capital Expenditures

= Free Cash Flow

10-K and 10-Q: The 10-K and 10-Q documents generally detail any other financial information that you may be looking for. In these documents, you can find an auditor's report, any management discussion, and analysis (MD&A), along with other less sought after data.

10-Ks are submitted annually and provide a glimpse of the business' performance over the course of a full fiscal year. You can look back at a company's history by reviewing the 10-Ks for any number of years in the past. If you're not familiar with the 10-K, you probably know it by its other term, the Annual Report. While the two are not exactly the same, they do cover the same material, but the Annual Report is basically the same information but in a different format, which is much easier to read.

The 10-Q however, is just a smaller snapshot of the 10-K as it only covers a quarter of the filing year. There are only 3 10-Qs released each year. The fourth quarter report is always included in the 10-K filing at the close of the year.

The Management Discussion and Analysis (MD&A)

Another useful fundamental analysis tool is the MD&A. It is usually used as a preface to the financial statements and contains a synopsis of what you will find within each of the documents. You can learn more about what the company does and the primary areas where the company has done well for that period of time.

Basically, it is the manager's analysis of the company's performance, so it will not go into extensive detail about the good, the bad, and the ugly, but it will give you a pretty good glimpse of what to expect.

The Auditor's Report

The Auditor's report gives the opinion on the accuracy of any of the financial statements and discloses any additional information they may feel necessary to share. Every public company must have their annual reports audited by an independent CPA firm. The auditor combs over the reports and scrutinizes every detail looking for anything that might compromise the integrity of the data.

Footnotes to the Financial Statements

Footnotes in the financial statements are there to cover any additional details so that you have a clearer understanding of a company's position. These can include any additional information that may not have a place in the body of the document. For example, they might list outstanding debts, maturity dates, and compensation plans, etc.

There are two different types of footnotes:

• Accounting Methods, which explain accounting policies or procedures you may not be aware of.

• Disclosure could include anything that could not be included in the formal statement. Anything from specific calculations used, liabilities connected to pension plans or additional costs not listed in the main document.

While the three primary documents are essential for a good fundamental analysis, an informed investor will dig even deeper to find additional data that others might overlook.

How to Value a Stock

Now that you have accumulated all of your data, it's time to figure out how to use it to determine the value of a given stock. In the sections above, we have given you formulas to help you to determine the numbers you need to make a relatively trustworthy valuation but applying the numbers is a bit more complex.

You will first need to determine the company's Discounted Cash Flow (DFC). This will help you determine if the company's current value is, in fact, its true value, a representation of the present value of its future cash flows that can be attributed to its shareholders.

$$DCF = CF_1/(1+r)^1 + CF_2/(1+r)^2 + CF_n/(1+r)^n$$

CF = Cash Flow R + discount rate (WACC)

Let's try to break this down into more manageable pieces. Let's say that we are confident that the company can generate $1/share in cash flow for every year in the foreseeable future. With this information, we can determine just what this type of cash flow is worth in today's market. We can then take that value and compare it to the company's present value and use it to determine if the company has been over or undervalued.

To do this, there are several different methods to use to value a discounted cash flow. Each method differs based on the type of cash flow used. When using the Dividend Discount Model, it will focus on company dividends while the cash flow formula will analyze the cash paid to shareholders after all expenses have been met.

This, however, becomes more complex when you consider that the model you're using involves a large number of estimates and assumptions. Forecasting a company's revenues and expenses over a period of five to ten years can be extremely complex. However, the DCF formula is a very practical and valuable tool that most analysts and investors learn to rely on.

The first step in determining the DCF analysis is to decide just how far into the future you want your cash flow projections to be.

The Forecast Period: Since the majority of companies are not able to grow at a faster rate than the economy for an extended period of time, you will have to estimate the length of your forecast period and how long the excess returns will continue. To do this, investors usually will use the company's current competitive and market position to venture an educated guess. Below are some basic guidelines you can use to come to a realistic conclusion.

Competitive Position Forecast Period

If the company that is growing slowly:

Highly competitive Low margin industry 1 Year

If it is a strong company:

Strong marketing Brand recognition Regulatory advantage 5 Years

If the company has exception growth:

High barriers to entry Dominant marketing position Many prospects 10 Years

Once you have your forecast period, you can start working on an estimate of the Free Cash Flow Growth for that timeframe.

Step 1: Forecast Revenue Growth

Let's assume that we are working with a strong company, so we've decided on the Five-Year Forecast. We now have to think about the company as a whole as well as the industry and how it will look five years into the future. Is the business or the industry going to grow, or will it start to shrink? What is its market share? Are there any new products or services coming that will drive the sales up?

Admittedly, much of this is guesswork at its best, but it can still be beneficial, especially if you can imagine the company in a variety of scenarios.

So, for demonstration purposes, we'll look at two ways to do this; one presenting a positive future and the other using extreme caution. Let's assume that the company's annual revenues come to $100 million. Your forecast model would look something like the chart below.

Formula #1: Positive Growth Potential

Current Year - $100 million Year 1 - $120 million (assuming 20% growth for each year) Year 2 - $144 million Year 3 - $172.8 million Year 4 - $207 million Year 5 - $248.9 million

Formula #2: Conservative Growth Potential

Current Year $100 million Year 1 $120 million (assuming 20% growth for years 1 and 2) Year 2 $144 million Year 3 165.6 million (assuming 15% growth for years 3 and 4) Year 4 190.4 million Year 5 $209.5 million (assuming only 10% growth)

Now that the forecasts are completed, you need to estimate the Free Cash Flow over the same time period. Remember, you have to go back to the reports in order to figure out the different calculations for the Free Cash Flow formula:

Sales Revenue Less Operating Costs Less Taxes Less Net Investment Less Change in Working Capital

= Free Cash Flow

Now, it is just a matter of putting it all together to calculate the Free Cash Flow.

Determining the Discount Rate

The next step in the valuation process is to find the discount rate, which can be used to calculate the Net Present Value of the cash flows. There are several methods used to do this, but one good method is to use what is called the Weighted Average Cost of Capital or the WACC, which is a mix of the equity costs and the after-tax cost of the company's debt.

There are two primary sources where a company can find financing – through debt or through equity. The WACC consists of the average cost the company has on hand to raise the money. This is calculated by taking the cost of the capital source (debt + equity) and multiplying it by its weight and then adding the sums together.

$$E/V * Re + D/V * Rd * (1 - Tc) = WACC$$

Re = the cost of equity Rd = the cost of debt E = the market value of the company's equity D = the market value of the company's debt

E + D = V

E/V = percentage of financing in equity

D/V = percentage of financing in the debt

Tc = the corporate tax rate

As you calculate the WACC, first determine the proportion of the company that has been financed through equity and how much is financed by debt. Do this by entering their respective values into the equation. Then determine the portion of equity and multiply it by the cost of the equity (Re), and the portion of debt should be multiplied by the cost of the debt (Rd).

You will notice that there are two sides to the equation. The debt side (*Rd) is multiplied by (1-Tc). This will give you the after-tax cost of the debt. Finally, you add the equity side to the debt side of the equation to get the WACC.

The final calculation needed is to determine the Terminal Value of a stock. With the Free Cash Flow forecast, you can estimate the actual value of the company's cash flow for the period.

Terminal Value = final project year cash flow * (1 + long-term cash flow growth rate)/(discount rate − long-term cash flow growth rate). This will adjust our figures to give us a Terminal Value for the company.

Total Enterprise Value

To get the total company value, or what is sometimes referred to as the Enterprise Value (EV), take the current value of the Cash Flow and divide it by the discounted rate, and then add the results:

Finally, you want to find the Fair Value of Equity. This will incorporate the company's debt. Most investors are very interested in separating the value of the shares out, so they can deduct the Net Debt from the Enterprise Value to determine the Fair Value of the Company's equity.

Fair Value = Enterprise Value less the Debt

Congratulations! You have now completed your first Fundamental Analysis. If you find that the shares are currently trading below their true value, it could mean a great buying opportunity for you. On the other hand, if it is trading at too high a value, it may be time to sell.

This is not a quick calculation and it is important to make sure that every step is done correctly. If it is too complex for you, you can easily use many of the online analysis tools where you only have to input the numbers to get the results you need. One formula you can use is the Gordon Growth Model (also referred to as the Dividend Discount Model).

How to Read Stock Quotes

One of the reasons why beginning investors gravitate to the price of stocks is because it is the only thing on a stock quote they can understand. The terms, references, labels, and even the format can sometimes be confusing. Reading a stock quote can be like trying to read a cup of tea leaves. Even some who have been trading for many years have to stop and try to make sense of all the information it contains. But once you've mastered the basics below, the quote itself won't seem so difficult to master.

Format

Regardless of where you find the stock quote, it will have a similar format so whether you're looking in a newspaper or you've found it online, they will all have the same basic information and look the same with just a few small variations. At the very least they should have the name of the company and its ticker symbol (the one to three-digit symbol indicating which stock it is).

It should also give you some indication of where you can go to buy the stock. For example, it might show NYSE, meaning you can purchase the stock on the New York Stock Exchange or NASDAQ.

Below this, there are usually two columns, each filled with a lot of numbers. The column on the left focuses on basic numerical facts about the stock while the column to the right gives you numbers relating to analyzing the stock.

Last Trade

The Last Trade tells you the most recent price that was paid for a single share of the stock. This number changes very quickly. You'll probably notice it changing right before your eyes depending on where you find the information. Some sites will update live while others will update every 1 - 5 minutes.

Trade Time

Another piece of information that will be valuable to you is the trade time or the time the last trade took place. It will help you determine how long it's been since the price was updated. The price you're looking at may have already changed as it is quite common for the system to be a few minutes behind real time. So, if you see that there has been a longer lapse in time since the last quote, it may be time to get an update.

Change

This indicates the difference between the last trade and the trade before that. It basically only details the movement of the stock within the last few minutes and has no real reflection on the overall history of the stock's performance.

Prev. Close

Another important indicator of a stock's performance is the Previous Close. This is the price of the final trade of the previous day sold for. It's like a snapshot of one sale in a 24-hour period, but it does not give you a real picture of a stock's history or current movement. If you're planning on getting in and out of the market within a short period of time, this information may prove useful to you.

Open

The price that the first share sold at for the current day.

Bid & Ask

The Bid is the highest price that someone is willing to pay for a single share and the Ask is the lowest price that someone is willing to accept.

1y Target Est

This number is an analysts' projection of what the price will be for a single share of the stock one year from the present. This is one area of the stock quote that can vary widely depending on the analyst who wrote it. There are so many variables that can come into play when projecting future prices that no two people will come with the same projections. Only use this number as an educated guess and don't put too much emphasis on it for investment decisions.

Day's Range

The Day's Range can give you an idea of how the stock moved for that particular day. Consider it to be a larger picture of how well the stock has traded. 52-WK Range

This is similar to the day's range but extends it to include the range over the course of the last year. If the stock is very volatile, the Day's Range will probably give you a more accurate picture of price movements but for more stable and consistent stocks, the 52-WK Range may serve you better.

Volume

The volume is the total number of shares that changed hands throughout the course of a single day. If it is an extremely active stock, then you'll want to figure out why there is so much movement. This kind of activity could be a reflection of bad news, causing many to sell or good news that triggers a major buying spree.

Avg. Vol

The average volume gives you the average volume over a set period of time. It could be for a day, a few months or for as much as a year. Knowing the average volume of a stock can be very useful in helping you decide when the volume is active enough for you to get in or out of the market.

Market Cap

The Market Capitalization gives you an approximate dollar value of the entire stock of a company being traded. The figure is determined by multiplying the total number of shares by the price of the last trade.

P/E

This is the price to earnings ratio showing the relationship between the price of a single share of stock and the income the company has earned for that share. The higher the P/E ratio the more expensive a stock will be.

EPS

The Earnings per Share is the total amount an investor would have earned if he had purchased a single share of the stock in the last quarter and sold it at that specific time. This can be a valuable tool giving you insight into how a stock will do if an investor plans to sell it in the near future. However, this figure is not very useful to long-term investors who plan to hold for an extended period of time.

Div & Yield

For investors interested in dividends, the dividend and yield are likely going to be the most valuable piece of information you can get from a stock quote. The dividend is the payment you receive from the company for holding onto a single share of stock. The yield is the amount of the dividend shown as a percentage of the price for a single share.

Beginning investors tend to look at the high price of a dividend when it is actually better to look at the yield. An extremely high yield can be an indication that the company is having difficulties.

When it comes to choosing the perfect stock, there are many small details you need to evaluate. It is not enough to just get all the numbers about a particular stock in place, you should never forget that the stock you choose must also be compatible with your investment goals and fit well in your financial portfolio. For that reason, no one can tell you exactly how to pick the perfect stock for you.

Bull and Bear Markets

Finally, there are two more terms you hear quite frequently in stock investment circles. A Bull or Bear market can definitely influence not just which stock to invest in but when to make the investment.

If you get a little confused about these references, keep in mind that a bull is a fierce animal that attacks by thrusting its head and its horns up, thus goring its prey. When it is a Bull market, the price of the stocks is on the rise. A bear, on the other hand, generally attacks its prey by taking its claws and striking down, so in a bear market, the price of the stocks is generally on a decline.

The degree to which the market rises or falls can vary greatly, but it is safe to assume that if it is declared a bull or a bear market, that the price movements are extreme, often as much as 20% or more. In order for it to be declared a bull or bear market, this extreme movement must happen across several indexes and not just in one area.

These types of markets generally appear as a

result of major changes in larger economic patterns happening in the world. For example, a Bull Market is usually an indication that investors are confident in the economic growth of their community while a Bear Market usually indicates a growing fear that the economy is not doing very well.

Taking advantage of a Bull Market can produce amazing results for you over the years. For example, if you had invested $1,000 in the S&P 500 at the start of the Bull Market 30 years ago, your investment would now be worth $7,600 today. It's definitely something worth considering.

Learning how to analyze stocks, pick the right ones for your portfolio, and predict stock movements is at the heart of stock market investing. Some of the information included in this chapter will need to be read several times in order for you to get the full sense of it. However, if you put in the extra brainpower to master these skills, you can reduce your risk level exponentially and open the door to even more profits in the long run.

Chapter 5: What Are Index Funds?

One of the first places new investors tend to turn when starting in the stock market is Index Funds. They have become a very popular tool in the investment world. In fact, according to the latest statistics, at least $1 out of every $5 investment dollars finds its way into index funds.

So, what exactly is an Index Fund and why do you need to know about it? To understand this question, you first need to understand an index. An index is basically a compilation of specific guidelines developed by a group of people on how to build a portfolio of different stocks and bonds. Any stocks or bonds that fit within those guidelines is included in the index and becomes a part of the index fund.

For example, the most well-known index fund in America is the Dow Jones Industrial Average (DJIA). It is a group of thirty different blue-chip stocks that are considered to be the most important to the United States economy. Within the DJIA, the shares are weighted based on the price of the stock as well as for any adjustments that may be needed. The committee that compiles the DJIA is the editors of The Wall Street Journal. Any instruments included on this list must meet all the criteria of the committee before even being considered.

Historically, the DJIA has been very effective in choosing profitable stocks. It has repeatedly beaten other well-known indices, including the most discussed index in the world, the Standard & Poor's 500 (S&P 500).

Difference between an Index Fund and a Mutual Fund

Many people tend to get the terms index fund and mutual fund confused. An Index Fund is a mutual fund that does not use a portfolio manager to make decisions about trades. This task is in the hands of the committee or group that sets up the guidelines. For example, the DJIA is managed by the editors of the Wall Street Journal. So, if you choose to buy a share in the DJIA, you're really turning your money over to the editors of the Wall Street Journal and trusting them to decide which stocks to invest in. The same is true for any other index fund you choose. You will, however, still own a percentage of shares in each of the stocks on the index; you're just pooling your resources and trusting the managing party with which stocks to put into your portfolio.

Benefits of Index Funds

Historically speaking, index funds do tend to outperform other analysts when it comes to generating profits, so if you do not have the time to research each individual stock for yourself, there is a pretty good chance that you will do well with them. In addition to saving you a lot of time, there are many other advantages to investing in index funds, especially for those who do not have a lot of money to spare.

Lower Cost: One of the biggest attractions is their lower cost. Think of it as a collection of hundreds and sometimes thousands of stocks all collected together. If you were to invest in each stock individually, it would probably cost you a small fortune, something that newer investors do not usually have. For example, the S&P 500 is a collection of 500 of the largest companies in the United States. Just buying into one of these stocks (Amazon for example) where a single share is over $1,900 might eat up every dollar you have to invest. However, by purchasing 1 share of the S&P 500, you get a piece of that Amazon shares added to your portfolio.

It gives you instant diversification with one single investment that would cost you a fraction of the time and money you have set aside to build your financial portfolio.

Tax Efficient: Index funds are also very tax efficient in that they don't require you to do a lot of trading. Since managers are not constantly trading back and forth on your behalf, you are not hit with a lot of earnings that could be susceptible to taxes. This can also translate into more money to keep in your pocket. If you were doing a lot of individual trades, you would also be hit with a number of trading fees as well as excessive management fees that could easily cut into your returns.

Lower Risk: Index funds tend to be lower risk because there is fewer turnovers in the market. A low turnover has historically been one of the most effective ways of generating money in the market. Statistics have repeatedly shown that those investors that do best in the market have often invested in individual stocks and simply held onto them for the long-term. Buying into index funds and holding them for the long-term has often produced much more profitable results without the associated risks that often come with constant buying and selling.

Proven Performance: Undoubtedly, just as there are different types of stocks, some good and some bad, the same can be said of index funds. However, when looking at those funds that have had performances higher than those of individual investors, the message is very clear.

For example, the average rate of return from the S&P 500 Index over the decade ending in December of 2012 was around 7.10%. The Fidelity and Vanguard funds did almost equally as well with returns around 6.99 and 7.03%.

Of course, when you invest in these funds there are no concrete guarantees that the funds will pay but historically speaking, their performances generally do outperform the strategies of other systems. The trick here is to choose a fund where you can understand how each stock is chosen. That way, you can better predict its performance over the years.

Cost vs. Risk: Warren Buffet, probably one of the world's most successful investors, is a strong believer in index funds. His view is that both large investors and small investors should have some portion of their portfolio in index funds.

This is primarily because there is very little risk associated with them. This is one of the primary reasons why financial advisors are so enthusiastic about them. As far as costs go, they are likely the least expensive means of investing. Your costs are minimal when compared to paying fees to financial managers so that they can reap huge profits as well.

The average fee you may pay for an index fund is between 0.08 to 0.12%, which is significantly less than paying a manager outright.

In addition, you also save money in a less tangible way. Most new investors lose money because they are too emotionally connected to the market. Index funds remove that risk from you as the management team handles all the investment decisions about which stocks to include. They do all the research and valuations necessary to determine which stocks will make the grade and how much of your money will go into them.

How to Get Started

Getting started investing in index funds is rather simple. It's really just a matter of making a few simple decisions.

1. Decide which brokerage firm you want to work with. You're going to have to do that anyway, even if you don't decide on index funds. This publication is not endorsing or affiliated with any particular brokerage firms, but popular brokerage firms with good reputations include Charles Schwab, Vanguard and & Fidelity. Visit their respective websites to open a brokerage account and get started today!

2. Get a list of potential index funds offered and choose one. There are many

to choose from. You can decide based on sector, geography, or style.

a. Sector Indices are defined by a specific industry. These could include Energy, Materials, Industrials, Consumer Discretionary,

Consumer Staples, Health Care, Financials, Information Technology, Telecommunications, or Utilities.

b. Style Indices have style classifications. These could include things

like market capitalization, growth or company value.

c. Geographical Indices are those companies located in a specific

country or region.

To find out more about the different funds available, your broker should be able to provide you with a list of options that fit within your investment goals. 3. Check costs. Index funds can vary in cost, but they tend to be much lower than other investment options. This is mainly because they are not actively managed but run almost entirely on automation. There are several costs that you should make sure of before you decide.

a. Minimum investment required b. Minimum account balances required c. Expense ratio d. Tax-cost ratio

4. Finally, decide which index you want and make your purchase. Some popular index funds at the time of this publishing are The Charles Schwab S&P 500 Index (SWPPX) and the Schwab Total

Stock Market Index. (SWTSX) While we do not have any affiliation with these funds, they have been well reviewed consistently.

One final point to remember about Index Funds. Index funds can be a very easy investment tool and the returns can be incredible. But that doesn't mean that you should completely remove your interest in the equation. While you may not need to be monitoring its every move, you should keep enough interest in them to ensure that it is continuing to do the job you expected it to do. Look at the funds' returns on its quote page periodically and compare it to the benchmark you set in the beginning. This way, you can be sure that you're going to get the kind of results you're looking for and get the most out of your investment decision. For stock market investing beginners an index fund can be an ideal option.

Chapter 6: What are Mutual Funds?

At its very heart, a Mutual Fund is a stock or bond portfolio that is professionally managed. In the last chapter, we discussed index funds and mutual funds are similar but are actively managed instead of mirroring a stock market index. It is a means of pooling resources together from a large number of investors and investing in a collection of stocks that are linked together by purpose, geography, or some other common denominator.

While the end result is your ability to buy into certain stocks and bonds, there is one distinct difference when you invest in a mutual fund. Unlike when you buy shares in a certain company directly, you get a relative amount of voting rights. This is not the case with a mutual fund investment. This is primarily because investing in mutual funds is like investing in a large number of different stocks with one investment. In most cases, you will not own a full share of a company but only a partial one through the fund.

This does not mean that your earnings will be diluted in any way. You will still receive a proportional share of any returns that your investment earns. There are three primary ways that an investor can earn money through a mutual fund.

1. Money can be paid through stock dividends or through the interest paid on bonds maintained within the portfolio. Most funds will automatically reinvest the earnings to help in building up the profits earned over time.

2. Money can also be earned through capital gains from securities in the fund. These are usually passed on to investors in the form of a distribution.

3. If the instruments within the fund increase in price, then as an investor,

you have the option to sell your shares for a profit in the market.

There are some obvious advantages to Mutual Funds for new investors and some negatives that you should be aware of.

Benefits of Investing in Mutual Funds

• The biggest advantage is that your portfolio has a professional manager who will do all the research needed to trade on your behalf. They will be aware of certain stocks, bonds, and securities you may not even be aware of. It is by far, one of the easiest investment tools to get into and the ideal platform for most new investors to start investing in stocks.

- They automatically diversify your portfolio for you. This lowers your level of risk, spreading it out over a large array of holdings. Something that would be very difficult to do if you were investing in individual stocks.

- They offer lower fees because they have bulked your funds together with other investors so rather than paying a single transaction fee for every buy and sell, you add to your portfolio, you only pay a percentage of transaction fees made on your behalf.

- They are easy to buy. You can purchase mutual funds from any brokerage firms and most banks also have their own line of mutual funds. Many can be started for a minimum investment amount, some with as little as $100 as a starting point.

- They give you more variety. You can find mutual funds available in a wide variety of asset classes. They are not all rooted in stocks and bonds. You can also find Funds that trade in foreign currency, commodities, and even real estate. It opens the door to investment in other avenues you may not have considered before.

- Regulations are usually pretty strict when it comes to mutual funds. They are not only subject to regulation by the SEC, but they are also subject to several industry-related regulations all in place to ensure the protection of your investment.

Active or Passive Management

When choosing a Mutual Fund to invest in, you need to pay close attention to the type of management offered. There are two types to choose from – Active or Passive management. The decision you make should be based on your personal circumstances. Both types can be very advantageous to have in your financial portfolio. However, there are some distinct differences you need to consider. To decide, it is important that you know the difference between the two.

Passive Managers: A passive manager will automatically buy into all the instruments found on a particular Index. Funds with passive management typically have lower fees.

Active Managers: An active manager, on the other hand, has a more pick and choose a role. While he or she must purchase from the options on the list, he is not compelled to put a little money into all of them. As a result, the choices made will be based on which of those instruments meet with the investment strategy he is working on. Some of these managers will look for undervalued companies and others may be looking at performance expectations.

Active fund managers generally come with a higher cost because they are more involved in building up your portfolio. Your decision will depend on several things.

- The manager's past record of success

- Your budget

- Your investment goals

There are definitely advantages to both, but the final decision should be based on your personal needs and expectations. Keep in mind that even if you do find an excellent active manager to handle your fund, it is not likely to expect the same results over and over again. The stock market is very volatile and things can change very quickly so due to many variables, the results received for one period of time may not be repeated again. It is reasonable to expect some dips and valleys in your returns over the long-term.

Therefore, passive managers may be more affordable, but they don't usually return the high results that active managers do, but they are also less risky.

All of these things should be carefully considered before you decide to invest in a mutual fund of any kind.

As an example, to get started simply

research a popular mutual fund such as the T. Rowe Price Blue Chip Growth Fund (TRBCX) ,open a brokerage account and purchase shares! It's as simple as that! But be sure to do your research since investing has inherent risks and we are not in a position to make specific recommendations only to provide examples for the purposes of teaching investing!

Chapter 7: Learning to Read a Chart

There is definitely an art to making sense of the many charts and graphs used in following the movements of a stock. In order to be a successful stock investor, you need to accept these instruments as part of your new financial life. These economic indicators can prove to be invaluable when it comes to determining where a stock is headed. From these, you can learn not just the price of a stock, but its volume, its history, and a wealth of other information that would help you to recognize a good stock to invest in.

Chart Basics

To begin with, you need to understand exactly what the purpose of the chart is. It is an accurate record of how the stock has performed over a specified period of time. We all know that stock prices are not static, and they can constantly fluctuate up and down. There could be a major price swing as a reaction to the news in the media or as a result of a change in management within the company. In fact, there are many variables that are constantly at work at any given time affecting the price movements. One of the biggest secrets to success lies in your ability to figure out exactly what those movements mean.

New investors often conclude that price movement is unpredictable. After all, how can one individual investor know what millions of other shareholders are going to do at any given time? However, once you realize that many movements are predictable, and it is just a matter of mass psychology, then you will begin to trade with more confidence and tap into one of the greatest wealth building strategies the world has ever seen.

While you have already learned the basics of fundamental and technological analysis, these alone are only the beginning of stock investing. The other half of the puzzle is pinpointing exactly when a stock is in the right position to trade or finding out if the stock is at the right price.

Unlike in the past, charts for just about any stock on the market are readily available and most of them can be found at no cost. Of course, some charts are easier to navigate than others, but learning how to use them will help you to effectively follow thousands of stocks online with just a few taps of your computer keyboard.

How to Use Chart History

We have said it before; the past performance of a stock is never a guarantee of continued

performance but that does not mean that you can't
learn

from following a stock's history. In fact, history is probably the easiest thing to figure out on a chart.

When it comes to the history of a stock, there are seven basic factors that seem to repeat themselves over and over again among many of the best- performing stocks throughout history. By learning these seven basic fundamentals, you build for yourself a foundation that you can use to measure and analyze any potential stock that you may be interested in investing in.

But before you get into studying individual stocks, you need to take a look at the big picture. The market as a whole operates in cycles. Over the more than 100 years of stock market investing, the US stock market has gone through a never-ending series of peaks and valleys. It is true that the market has increased exponentially over the years, but it has not gotten to where it is today by going in a straight line. What we've witnessed are those extremely high highs and unbelievably low lows with an overall average of about 10% return year over year.

Understanding a Market Cycle: One of the first things you'll learn when looking at chart history is how to read the market cycles. Just mastering this fundamental can open the door to huge returns.

Most people have heard references to a

market bubble and even if they don't know what it really means, they are sure they don't want to be caught in one. Yet, every cycle, people still find themselves caught in one because they don't recognize the beginnings and the ends of a cycle.

A bubble is simply one type of market cycle. In fact, there are four different phases of a market cycle. During each of these phases, you can expect certain things to happen. Learning to identify which phase of a cycle you're in can help you to avoid getting into the market at the wrong time.

• Accumulation Phase: starts after the market has hit bottom and investors are starting to buy into a certain stock. This is a time when people believe that the worst is over and it is safe to buy again. At this point, valuations are extremely attractive because the general sentiment throughout the market is still more on the bearish side. General attitudes are slowly beginning to shift from negative to neutral.

• Markup Phase: At this point, people are beginning to notice that the market has stabilized and the valuations are starting to increase. More people will begin to tentatively enter the market and as a result, higher lows and higher highs will begin to appear. The sentiment is shifting again to a more optimistic view. Later in this phase, market volumes will increase and valuations will start to climb to uncommon norms. The overall sentiment now is bullish.

• Distribution Phase: At this phase, sellers have full control of the market. Prices are locked into a trading range that could last for just a few weeks or extend for months at a time. Those investors who have been sitting on the sidelines are now flooding the market and emotional investors are in force being spurred on by a fear of missing out (FOMO) and greed. Valuations are at all-time highs, but the market cannot sustain these elevated prices for long.

• Mark-Down Phase: In this final phase, the market begins to reverse. Many emotional investors will hold on to their investments, hoping that the price will recover and they can at least break even. By the time the market has plunged more than 50%, they finally let go, giving up their investment as lost. Sadly, this is the time for the smart investor to buy, as this is when the market is at its bottom. Those that do are poised to take advantage of the next accumulation phase.

Understanding a market cycle is the key to being able to time the market correctly. There is no set time limit for a cycle, it could last for a few weeks or it could last for years.

Yes, markets can go up and down every hour

and every day, but each of those small fluctuations does not actually mean it has gone through a cycle. One way you can be sure it is a cycle is to look at the charts. If the market has suffered the kind of decline in prices overall, one that takes a year or more to recover from, you are probably looking at a market cycle. One of the first things you need to learn is the seven different ways to identify a market cycle.

1. Look at the length: Market cycles vary in length. Some could last as

little as a year while others could last a decade or more.

2. Look at the valuations: When you see valuations like the P/E or P/S ratios changing and showing different extremes, it could be evidence of a market cycle. Valuations may be consistent in one cycle but when a new market cycle begins, these will quickly change.

3. Look at already identifiable cycles: It is not uncommon to see a cycle form within an existing cycle. Smaller cycles will affect different types of stocks. For example, value stocks may be affected in one cycle, but growth stocks may fare differently. These smaller cycles could be industry exclusive as well.

4. Look at interest rate conditions: The environment that surrounds interest rates can affect every market cycle in a completely different way.

When bank interest rates are low, it is a good environment for stocks. So, if you see the rates in a decline, expect to see a bull market on the rise. On the other hand, when you see the rates on the rise, there will be an opposite effect on the stocks.

5. Do not confuse a market cycle with an economic cycle: A market cycle is an indicator of what investors will pay for shares in a company's stock, while the nation's economic cycle indicates how the economy is growing. The two may influence each other but since they measure different things, don't expect them to correlate exactly.

6. Buy in a bear market: It can be very exciting when you watch stocks moving in a continuous upward movement. It can be very difficult to sit patiently and wait for the cycle to come to an end so you can buy in. However, buying when the stocks are low can be very critical when it comes to making money.

7. When a cycle comes to an end: A crash usually comes at the end of a cycle and psychologically, you'll see investor sentiment take a turn for the worse. What was once excitement and anticipation of what is to come, generally turns to fear of impending doom. The dread that disaster is imminent can cause people to pull out of the market rather than take advantage of the many deals found

at the market lows.

All of these little observations should teach you several things. First, it is not easy to time the market – mainly because it is not always easy to identify a market when you're in the middle of it. However, it should also teach you that discipline is the key to success in stock market investing.

Keep in mind that market cycles, while they are a fundamental of this type of investment, are driven primarily by psychology, which could be either extreme fear or extreme greed. As long as you can refrain from these types of emotions, you should be able to enter and exit the market in a rational way, allowing you to tap into those times that could prove to be most profitable.

The best way to understand these things is by looking at chart history. While there is no guarantee that history will repeat itself, it can help you to understand the psychology that drove the market in the past, so you can reasonably expect it to repeat itself sometime in the future.

Patterns and Precedents

Charts are basically economic indicators that are carefully plotted on graphs so that they can be analyzed and interpreted. Just about anything can be charted from a stock's price to its volume. As these things are plotted, their

activity leaves behind a very visible pattern that can tell you if a stock is strong, healthy, or about to falter.

Because the stock market as a whole is just a huge auction block, the power of supply and demand becomes a huge factor in trading. The patterns that appear on these charts will show you specific price corrections and consolidations as they happen. You need to master the skill to learn these patterns and how to analyze them, so you can make informed decisions about your investments.

Many would assume that stock market investing is economically driven but we've already learned that it is more about group psychology than anything else. Everyone is looking for some type of gain, some are fearful of losing what they have, others are thinking about taxes, hedging, fundamentals, the advice they've received, and lots more. Your ability to gauge the psychology of those who are throwing their money in the pot with you is right there on the charts.

You can learn a lot from analyzing chart patterns. Once you've been able to master them, an amazingly clear picture begins to emerge; a historical record of every trade and every thought of others interested in the same stocks. This information, once deciphered, can provide you with a framework that you can use to figure out whether it is the bears or the bulls in control at any given point. The more you understand about charts and what they say, the better you can position yourself for profit.

One of the main reasons why chart analysis is so effective is because people are highly predictable. The way the masses react to certain conditions is consistent throughout history. Once you learn the precedents set in the chart patterns, you'll see them reemerge time and time again making these valuable tools you can use to help you predict future movements that you can take advantage of. While there are a lot of patterns that can appear in charts, we'll look very carefully so that every investor should know how to identify and understand.

Cup and Handle: One of the most common chart patterns you will see is the "cup and handle." You can easily identify this pattern as it looks pretty much like it sounds. These patterns develop over as few as seven weeks but have been known to last as long as sixty-five weeks. On average, you will see the cup and handle pattern take somewhere from three to six months to form.

As you examine the chart, you will first notice the cup shape in the form of a "U" and the handle looks more like a downward slant coming off of the top of the cup. Any stock showing this pattern is subject to selling pressure from its investors. This pattern is generally seen as a buying trigger and helps investors to identify new opportunities to buy.

When analyzing the cup and handle pattern, there are certain characteristics that you should look for; each one will tell you something different about how the stock is performing.

• Length: Some cups will have a longer "U" shaped bottom, which is a strong buy signal.

• Shape: It is best to avoid any cups with a more "V" shaped bottom.

• Depth: Avoid trading if the cup is overly deep.

• Volume: Make sure the volume decreases or increases along with the price so that it stays lower than the average in the base of the bowl.

When you trade the cup and handle, make sure you set your stop and buy order just above the upper trend line on the handle. This way, your order is only executed if the price breaks the resistance level. You could also wait and close above the upper trend line by placing a limit order directly below the breakout level.

To set your target for profits, measure the distance from the bottom of the cup to the point where the price breaks out from the pattern and then extend the distance up to match the difference. For example, if the distance from the bottom to the breakout point is 20, then you would extend the line an additional 20 points above the handle. You can set your stop-loss orders right below the handle in case the price goes down.

It is normal for a growing stock to develop this pattern when the general market declines. It is also perfectly normal for a correction to happen 1½ to 2½ times the overall market averages. Keep in mind that any time the stock experiences a decline that is more than 2½ time its average, it should be treated with caution. These are often too wide or too loose and could, therefore, be destined for failure.

When this pattern corrects, you will usually see a drop from the peak (the top) to the bottom range anywhere from a low point of 12-15% all the way up to 33%. Make sure that the uptrend is very clear before the beginning of the base. Expect to see a 30% or more increase in price BEFORE the uptrend.

Cup patterns are very common in growth stocks, especially when there is a decline in the general market. Look for these in those stocks with base patterns that tend to deteriorate when the general market is on a decline.

After extensive research on this pattern, there are a few things you can learn:

- Stocks that form new highs straight from the bottom of the cup tend to be riskier because there is no pullback.

- A price that drops more than 50% from a peak to a low requires that it must increase more than 100% to reach a new high. Stocks in this position generally have a failure rate of 5-15%.

The handle area usually forms over a period of one or more weeks and the price tends to drift downward. This is called a shakeout; a point when the price drops to a point lower than initial low formed by the handle. You should see a noticeable drop in the price during the pullback phase. In most cases of a bull market, you shouldn't see an increase in volume during the correction phase.

When the price drops in the handle section, it should not exceed 12% of its peak when there is a bull market. Any drop that exceeds this point will form a wide and erratic pattern and is clear evidence that it is a high-risk possibility.

Pivot Points

As you examine this pattern, look for the pivot points (or the line of least resistance) where the volume for the day shows an increase of 40% or more above the normal. It is at these points where a breakout or a price reversal could happen. It is quite common to see these sorts of breakouts with percentages that could reach very high (200, 500, or even 1000% or more). These kinds of volume increase are usually the result of institutional buys and not individual investors.

Your goal though is not to buy at the lowest possible price, but to find the right time to buy. This means that you must watch these movements, wait for the price to reach the ideal buy point before entering your position. If you attempt to buy before the crucial pivot point, the stock may never break out. It could stall and start a pullback and you will lose a percentage of your investment. These pivot points are essential tools that can prove that a stock is strong and is a good opportunity. On the other hand, if you wait too long, you enter the market too late and could lose out with the next price correction.

Volume Clues

When you see the volume of a stock experience a major dry up that lasts for a week or more, it is usually an indication that the selling period of the cycle has come to an end. This is a common occurrence with any healthy stock in an accumulation phase, and it is likely the result of price fluctuations that are too small. This drying up of volume at key points on the chart can be very useful in your analysis.

Other clues to look for when it comes to volume are the appearance of daily or weekly spikes. These spikes that seem to appear right out of nowhere could be setting the stage for future runups. If you use a daily chart service like Daily Graphs Online from Investor's Business Daily along with weekly graphs, you'll be able to spot this unusual activity that may only happen once in a day.

The more you pay attention to the volume movements in conjunction with price movements, the clearer the picture will become. You will be able to identify the points where the stock falls under accumulation, which is a clear sign of institutional buying. Then, you will be able to make your own analysis of stock performance and no longer have to rely on the professional opinion of analysts or make those bungling mistakes based on faulty reasoning.

Market Corrections (What They Are)

If you think of the stock market in terms of numbers, then you miss about 80-90% of the thrust of the market movements. The vast majority of movements in charts are reflections of market corrections.

Basically, a market correction is a movement that reverses a previous movement. As you examine the charts, you may see a drop in the price of 10% or more, but this should not be a reason for discouragement. Instead, view it as an opportunity to take advantage of some good deals at a highly discounted price.

As you grow in your ability to analyze charts, you'll soon learn how to predict a market correction by comparing one market index to another similar one. With this technique, you can discover when a stock or index is underperforming and therefore, will need to be adjusted.

When a correction happens in an index, the individual stocks within it may be strong so it can prove to be the ideal time to get in and swoop up those assets that may not be performing to their full potential.

Other Common Patterns to Look for

Saucer with Handle: This price pattern is very similar to the cup and handle, but the saucer part of the pattern usually is stretched out and covers a much longer period of time. This makes the pattern shallower.

Double-Bottom: This pattern looks more like the letter "W" on the charts. You may not see it as often as you might see the cup and handle, but it will appear frequently enough to give you a clear sign of what to expect.

The key characteristics to look for with the double bottom are that the second bottom (the low) matches the first bottom in depth or that it drops slightly below it (only 1 or 2 points). This movement will shake out the weaker and less experienced investors.

You could see double-bottoms with handles but not always. The depth of this pattern will be similar to the depth in a cup pattern.

When you see the double bottom, your signal to buy is usually at the top right side of the W as the stock rises to form the recovery side of the second leg down.

Flat-Base: The flat-base pattern appears as a second-stage base where the stock has moved up more than 20% away from the cup and handle, saucer with handle or the double bottom. The base has a sideways movement keeping the price within a pretty tight range and maintains that level for five or six weeks with no major market corrections.

If for some reason, you miss out on the initial breakout, keep on the lookout for this flat-base, which will give you another chance to get in on the market at a discounted price.

Flags: Flag patterns, although rare, do occur from time to time. A high- tight flag may begin when the stock price moves up 100% or more within a very short period of time (maybe four to eight weeks). Then, it will show a sideways correction between 10-25%, which will develop during a period of three to five weeks.

As a bear market is about to end, a negative flag may seem to be developing. This happens when a strong stock breaks out of its base and rises. If it is not able to reach a 20-30% increase, it will have a pullback and start another sideways price consolidation directly above the previous base.

When the bear market ends, the stock will likely be one of the first to forge a new path to greater gains. Once the pressure from the overall market is removed, the stock will break free and eventually push up to even higher highs.

Relative Price Strength

The relative price strength is a method of measuring the trend of a stock. You can calculate the relative price strength by taking the price of one stock and dividing it by the price of another. For example, you might measure the stock of two similar companies against each other. As of this writing, Ford shares were priced at $9/share and General Motors is priced at $34/share. If you want to find the relative strength of Ford you would calculate ($9/34).

This information could be very useful when comparing the current relative price strength to previous calculations to see in which direction the company you're interested in is moving. It is not enough to know the relative price strength of the stock you're interested in, but you should also know how they are performing against their competition and the market overall.

For new investors, learning to master the basics of chart analysis is even more important. These are the same tools that professional investors have been using for many years as a means of finding new opportunities, identifying danger zones, and mastering the ability to time the market at the right time.

Stock market investing is not like bargain shopping. There is much more involved and the more you can capitalize on these tools, the easier it will be, and the more confidence you'll have in your investment decisions.

Chapter 8: How Important is History

The history of the stock market has been a perfect picture of the evolution of the financial growth of America. Around 200 years ago, our colonial government found that selling bonds were a great way to support the war effort. Later, private banks issued stocks to help companies raise money.

But it wasn't until 1792 that we saw the stock market begin to evolve into what it is today. It was then that 24 of the nation's largest merchants decided to join forces. They met daily on Wall Street and traded bonds and stocks. Those 24 merchants eventually became known as the New York Stock Exchange (NYSE).

By the mid-1800s, there was an economic boom in the nation. Investors anxiously wanted to find ways to get a piece of the fortunes that were being handed out. Companies began to offer stocks in earnest. These continued to grow until they reached a point where millions of dollars were being traded on a daily basis. Today, these all have had a major impact on not just individual investors' bottom line but the global economy as a whole.

Any country where the economy is strong will have a stock market that is steadily rising. This means that share prices are also increasing, all of it inadvertently impacting the individual wealth of everyone concerned.

The fact is that history can teach us a lot about the stock market. Through its pages, you can learn how the stock market has capitalized on new industries, witnessed the demise of once faithful leaders, and with the right strategies, has turned paupers into princes. Still, experts warn that we should not put too much emphasis on history when predicting what the market will do. While we can learn a lot about past mistakes and successes in the market, the old adage "history repeats itself" is not always true. What we do know is human behavior can pretty much rely on the fact that there are certain events that will trigger panic, greed, and other emotions pretty consistently.

Trying to extrapolate historical returns for future forecasts can be extremely complicated. For example, a look at investors from the early 1910s shows that only a few of them had the insight to predict the coming of the biggest decade of war mankind had ever seen. During that century, the world witnessed two global wars, socialist revolutions, and a financial depression that nearly decimated many nations. All of these had a huge global impact on the economy and the stock market.

In many cases, complete recovery took more than half a century to happen. While these events have had a major impact on the market in the past, they don't actually mean a whole lot when it comes to individual analysis of the market in the future.

That being said, being able to analyze historical stock charts can help you decide which way you will trade. Studying historical market analysis for longer- term trades can help investors to position themselves well ahead of major market cycles. Learning how to analyze different events in history can help you to better understand current market conditions.

To start with, you need to know where to look in order to find reliable market information. You can start by looking for a history graph of the market ticker for any company or index you're interested in. These can be found online at sites like Yahoo Finance, Google Finance, or any other site that provides reputable stock analysis software. Simply plug in the market ticker symbol and let the database pull up the appropriate historical data you need.

Onlinc analysis softwarc is oftcn frcc but there are also some paid software programs like Amibroker that will download the entire history of the stock market or an individual stock to research. They can even scan the market for potential new opportunities you would otherwise overlook, but these programs can be costly for the new investor, especially if they are not planning to start investing huge sums of money right away.

Once you've collected all of the data, it is important that you use it in the right way. It doesn't matter if your approach is through technical or fundamental analysis, your ability to earn a profit lies in the ability to recognize future opportunities within the data and avoid repeating the same mistakes of the past.

To use historical data correctly, your goal should be the study of market behavior over a predetermined period of time. Valuable information you can glean from these reports or things like price fluctuations, volatility, and volume; anything that can be quantified and studied.

As you examine these reports, you will begin to get some insight into the inner workings of the company and the market and how they relate to each other. This can be very useful in assisting you to develop a workable plan or enhance your current strategy.

Some key points to look for:

• Market Insight: study the past behavior of the stock looking for specific characteristics that are consistently displayed. Make note of anything that can be considered out of the ordinary and endeavor to understand its trigger.

• System Development: Look for the when, what,

and how of each trade under certain market conditions. Check for starting points of a new trading system and try to identify a developed model of the active trades.

- Consistency: Look for the kind of trades that you have confidence in mimicking. Those where you can see how they have performed over time and what was the cause of any unexpected results.

While you cannot rely entirely on historical data to predict the future, you can see where mistakes were made and learn from them so that when similar situations occur in the future, you won't repeat them. Using historical data analysis requires discipline that when applied correctly can give you a level playing field moving into the future.

A Look at Some Successful Winners in the Stock Market

No matter how you look at it, last year, 2017, was a very historical year in stock market rallies. It has been declared by some analysts as the year of investment strategies that were almost entirely based on following the winners of the market. Traders made huge fortunes simply by buying those shares that were rising the fastest. In the end, the winners achieved a whopping 38% return, the strongest in nearly twenty years.

Some of the most successful winning stocks in recent years are names you're likely familiar with: Apple (APPL), Amazon (AMZN), Facebook (FB), and Microsoft (MCST). These stocks were considered to be extremely heavy lifters that carried their investors through the toughest of time.

One key factor you learn from this is that while the individual sectors make up the market, they are not equal in nature. Some sectors or asset classes have performed much better in rough market conditions than others. A close examination of the market's history will reveal that some sectors have been very effective in outperforming the market while others have not.

A close look at last year's results shows that sectors such as Internet Applications, Resorts and Lodging, Aerospace/Defense, and Healthcare were the clear winners in recent years.

▪ With a few exceptions, technology mastered the market last year with Facebook being the clear winner. At end of 2017, its stock prices were up a whopping 43% over the previous year's performance.

▪ In the resorts and lodging sector, Wynn saw a 47% increase. Hotels, casinos, and cruise lines had some of the best-performing stocks for the year showing that there is still a strong demand for travel and leisure activities. This is all in spite of the fact that new competitors like Airbnb have entered the market. It is still a strong sector to consider investing in.

• With the aerospace and defense sector receiving a great deal of backing from the government, companies like Boeing are seeing unprecedented increases up to more than 50%.

• Healthcare is another big winner. With a growing population of seniors, medical appliances and new biotech innovations have witnessed new subsectors get a life of their own in recent markets.

You'll also notice that there have been major losers historically in the market as well.

• Time has not been very kind to REITs in recent years. With commercial spaces dwindling, this sector has suffered many different setbacks, which have left them with incredible losses almost completely across the board. Described as the "retailpocolypse," most of the stocks in this sector have seen big losses.

• The auto parts sector has also suffered. An industry that once dominated the market, the introduction of new hybrid and electric vehicles have triggered a domino effect of losses. By the end of 2017, companies like Advance Auto Parts experienced as much as a 35% drop in value.

- The retail industry also suffered greatly. With consumer habits gradually changing, traditional retailers like Urban Outfitters suffered a 34% drop and other once leaders in the industry also saw major declines. Ross stores, for example, fell about 14% even in the most active sales period of the year.

- The oil and gas industry also saw a major decline in market activity. Superior Energy experienced a 39% drop in value over the course of just one year. The spiraling downtrend, while it has hit the bigger companies hard, even the smaller independent producers are beginning to lose their edge in the newly developing market.

As you analyze these historical reports, you will have to look deeper under the surface in order to find the data you need to make a decision. Remember, the market is not about the numbers – the numbers are merely a reflection of the reaction of the people who trade in it. So, as you compare similar stocks, you must make sure that you connect the dots; all those trades were a reaction to something in the news, in the media, or in the business world in general. So, don't just settle for learning what happened in the market. The true secret to tapping into the historical records of the stock market is to become a detective and figure out the triggering event, the reason why investors bailed on one stock and ran towards another.

Ideally, you want to look for areas where growth was accelerating, find out why, and then try to determine if you believe that growth will continue or not. It is those kinds of decisions that will help you decide if the historical evidence you have uncovered will be useful enough for you to carry it forward into next few months, quarters, and years.

Chapter 9: Look for Major Growth In Earnings

Growth rates in stocks are very important when it comes to good analysis. These give you a clear picture of the percentage of change of a stock after it has been affected by certain variables. For the investor, growth rates are evidence of the compounded annualized growth of dividends, earnings, and revenues among other things.

All companies report good earnings at one time or another. These earnings are a crucial part of letting you know which ones make up the best investment opportunities. However, it is not always easy to determine how accurate a company's earnings are being reported. Even if they are accurate, as an investor, you don't want to settle for just the reports from one single quarter as a basis for making an intelligent decision. So, as you analyze an earnings report, you will need to dig a little deeper to make sure that the data you're using can steer you in the right direction.

So, you're not just looking for earnings, but you're looking for a pattern of growth. At the very least, annual earnings reported should show a continuous increase in each of the preceding three years. So, if there is an increase in earnings in the first year, a drop in year two, and another increase in year three, this would not show a steady increase. You're looking for growth across the board in all three years. A consistent and steady growth, no matter how incremental, is the picture of a good stock with a high probability that the growth will continue for the foreseeable future.

The 25-50% Rule

So, what percentage of growth should you be looking for? Ideally, you want to see growth of at least between 25% - 50% or more. As an example, let's consider a study of the market between the twenty-year span of 1980-2000. The average growth rate of all outstanding stocks was about 26%. A closer look at the biggest winners during that time shows that at least 75% of them had positive growth rates for the three years preceding their big wins; some even showing 5 years of growth prior to their top results.

As an example, take the #1 company on the Fortune 500 this year, Wal-Mart. As of this writing, Wal-Mart has shown growth for five years running now and has been listed in the top 10 businesses for 8 out of the last 10 years. With more than $485 billion in revenue, they are clearly leading the pack. Still, with the amount of revenue generated, their profits were only 13.6 billion. So, you need to look closer and find their earnings per share, which were as follows:

- 2016 EPS/4.68

- 2017 EPS/4.61

- 2018 EPS/3.78

On the surface, with all that revenue, it seems like they are a good deal. To support your conclusion, you will find that they have had consecutive years of growth with 2016 showing total revenue of $484,028, 000, 2017 with 484,604,000, and 2018 with 495,012,000. However, their earnings per share each year have been on a steady decline showing that all that revenue is not finding its way into the shareholders' hands. Take this a step further, if possible, look at what analysts expect the revenue to be in the coming years and you'll have a pretty good picture as to whether you can reasonably expect to turn a profit with your investment.

Keep in mind that estimates by analysts are not a guarantee. They simply reflect what one person believes will be the case. You should still rely on the facts, which is the annual growth rate preceding the present day.

By following the 25-50% rule, you can shield yourself from potential losses from stocks that may otherwise show highly profitable earnings.

Stock Market Cycles

Occasionally, you will find yourself in either

a bull or bear market. It can be unpredictable as to how long these cycles last. However, throughout history, we've come to learn that a bull market usually lasts between two and four years, which are followed by a bear market (or a recession).

When a bull market starts, you will see a surge in the common growth stocks as they begin to reach for new highs. You can identify these stocks by their profits growing quarter after quarter, but still struggling under poor economic conditions. Because of the steady decline of market conditions and the growth of their profits, the P/E ratio will look very favorable to investors.

These types of stocks can be found in the most basic of sectors including automobiles, chemicals, paper, rubber, and steel. In fact, three out of four cyclical stocks experienced a major turnaround over time. A perfect example of this was in the automobile industry in the early '80s with two of the leading manufacturers, Chrysler and Ford.

When these cyclical stocks are showing promise, amazing growth results are possible. Finding cyclical stocks does not mean that they are extremely competitive companies. Often, the competitiveness doesn't even show until the demand for their product or service becomes evident. For example, after the rapid buildup of basic needs began to be met by Chinese businesses, US companies stepped up their efforts to curtail the outflow of revenue to the Chinese in major industries like chemicals, copper, oil, and steel.

Even though these are cyclical stocks, they do not always represent the true future of the market. In fact, some of the old favorites can actually be crippling the market simply by the sheer challenges of their size. Many may have grown too large to be able to adapt to market changes very quickly, keeping them from being very competitive in the modern world.

If in your research, your interest is peaked in a cyclical stock, look for an annual growth rate of 5% or more for at least two consecutive quarters in a row. These growth rates should also be sufficient enough to boost the results for the last year into a whole new high.

Chapter 10: How to Determine Market Direction

Analyzing stocks can be very tricky. With so many variables in play, you could find a stock that meets every rubric you set out for yourself and still make a wrong decision. This is not because your research was inadequate nor is it because you failed in your calculations. The reason basically comes down to only a few basic factors, but quite likely, it is because of an inability to predict the direction the market is going in. Even the best analysts have an analytical system to help them to determine exactly which direction the market is moving. In short, you need a set of guidelines to help you decide when the market trend is bullish, bearish, or about to reverse.

To take this even further, if you're in a bull or a bear market, you need to know where you are in that market. Your investment strategy will change depending on whether you're in the early stage of the trend or not. You need to understand the market better; is it behaving normally, on the rise, declining, or is it strong or weak? To get the answer to these questions, you need a strategy that will help you analyze the entire market in such a way that you can come to a logical and reasonable conclusion on which direction you need to go.

One of the best methods to determine market direction is to follow the daily charts of several different general market averages. But you have to know exactly what you are looking for. There are several characteristics that you must earmark for extra scrutiny.

The general market: the most commonly used indexes on the market. From these, you can get a clue as to how strong or weak the activity for each day has been. Those indexes include:

o the S&P 500 o the Nasdaq Composite o The Dow Jones Industrial Average o The New York Stock Exchange Composite

You can find these listed in the Investor's Business Daily along with charts that show the moving averages and Accumulation-Distribution Ratings (ACC/ DIS RTG), which details if the index is getting support for either buying or selling. Make it a habit to check these indexes on a daily basis so you won't miss anything. By regularly studying these charts, you'll become familiar with the index's normal behavior and will be able to identify when they have hit their top or their bottom.

It is also important to understand what a normal market cycle looks like; how it slowly reveals itself over time. The two most important cycles to learn are the bull and bear markets. These do not end very easily and have often been known to deceive you into thinking they are about to close before moving another few notches up or down on the charts. These fundamentals are crowd psychology at their best.

A bear market ends subtly, with most of the business sectors still on the decline. Part of the reason for this is that the stocks are in an anticipation mode. They have already been discounting economic, political, and global events for quite a while. Most new investors do not realize that the events that happen on the stock market do not happen after the fact but are actually reacting to what events mean to the nation as a whole. Bull markets, on the other hand, usually see a top off and stocks can actually take a downturn before a recession begins.

By analyzing historical charts, you will learn to identify these market cycles and their normal behavior, so you can see and anticipate what potentials lay on the horizon.

One of the key points you want to look for is the pivot point when the general market changes direction. If for example, you notice a significant loss in a stock portfolio, it will need to see an even more significant gain in order to reach the point where it breaks even. Keep in mind that your goal is not just to earn money but to keep as much of it as possible. To do this, it is important for you to study the charts and follow the general rules of the game.

Should You HODL?

It has long been believed that long-term investors make money by remaining fully invested no matter what happens to a stock. While this has netted great profits for many people, this approach is not always the best course of action.

There have been times when standing still through a bear market has yielded good results, but not always. The problem lies in the inability to determine at the very start just how bad the economic situation is going to get. It may be short-lived or it could last for weeks, months, and even years.

In a bear market, nearly all of the stocks will fall, but if the cycle only lasts for a short period of time, you could end up in a position that the company may not be able to recover from. While HODLing can prove profitable in some circumstances, if your fundamental analysis doesn't give you a clear indication that the stock will definitely recover within a certain time frame, it is probably best that you sell off at least a portion of your portfolio, placing the returns in another stock that has better potential.

This is true for any stock, even if they have historically been industry leaders. A good example of an industry leader taking a tumble from glory is the Coca-Cola stock. During the 80's and 90's, the company's stock did very well, following the market as predicted. However, with the start of a bear market in 1998, the stock began to slip into a downward spiral that lasted for more than two years taking a good portion of the investor's money with it.

The question as to whether to HODL or not is not always cut and dry. There are times when HODL is the best choice, but it should not be assumed that it's the best course of action in all situations.

Protecting Yourself from Loss

Just as knowing how to identify the dangers of a bear market is crucial to your success as an investor. You also have to know when you've milked your stock for all its worth. As you become better at identifying the signs that indicate a market peak, you should already have a strategy in place to vacate your position as soon as possible.

When the market peaks, it will likely only hover at that position for a short while, maybe only a few minutes or hours. At the first sign of a downtrend, be prepared to put at least a quarter of your portfolio into cash (selling your stocks), so that they do not get trapped in a spiraling downtrend.

One of the best ways to do this is to use limit orders. These are orders that instruct your broker to sell the stock at a set price. If you don't specifically request a limit order, your shares will be sold at the market price, which means they could very well be sold at a price much lower than you anticipated. When in a bear market, your main objective should be to position yourself so that you can get out of the market when needed without losing.

The romance of riding the stock waves through the peaks and valleys can sound very exciting but in real life, sticking around to save a fraction of a point could be detrimental to your financial health.

In a true bear market, an investor only has two choices: 1) sell and vacate his position or 2) go short. When you go short, you are virtually out of the game and should stay out until you are sure the bear market is over. In some cases, that could be as little as a few months, but it could last for years.

How to Tell if the Price is Peaking

That leaves us with a big question. How does an investor know when the price of a stock is peaking? One way to do this is by watching the top indexes and how they perform. By following them as they push through their trend, you will start to notice how the volume of the stock pushes its way upward from one day to the next. At the same time, the index will show smaller price increases over the day before.

The averages do not have to end lower for evidence of a price topping out. If you notice that the average spread between prices from one day to the next starts to get a little wider, then you should have a pretty good idea that the stock is reaching its maximum potential.

There will likely be normal liquidation as the stock reaches its peak, occurring over three to six days spread out over four or five weeks. This means that the market is going through a distribution. If you notice four to five days of this type of distribution, the general trend following this action is usually downward.

When you are looking at the peak of the overall market, know that you only have to find these indicators in one index. There is no need to wait to see them in all of the indexes to know that it's about to turn into a bear market. Just being able to observe these points can make a huge difference in knowing exactly when to exit the market.

How to Tell if a Rally Will Succeed

The same could be said if you're in a bear market and the stocks are on the rise. Usually, after the initial drop, the stocks will begin to rebound and rally. The question then becomes, how do you know if this is a short rally or that it will continue up the charts? Again, you need to be able to look for specific signs that will give you evidence one way or another.

• Usually, the first rally after a peak will fail. Most investors will continue to sell at that point. You'll notice this if you see any of the following occur:

o The index rises in price on the third, fourth, or fifth rally but the

volume is decreasing.

o The average makes a small jump in price in comparison to the

previous day.

o The market average recovers less than half of the previous drop.

Follow the Leader

Another valuable indication of changes in market trend can be done by studying the daily averages. It is only logical to assume that if the market has been continuously rising for several years that some type of correction is necessary. You will begin to see that many of the leading stocks will develop an abnormal pattern.

This unusual activity can be observed in breaks in their chart formations as the price continues to go up. Price fluctuations will begin to appear that are oddly wider and looser than before. To get a better idea of this, take the time to study some of these older chart's daily and weekly histories.

You could also notice the leading stock will start to climb much faster for several weeks in a row. The price will break from the top when there is heavy volume and will suddenly be unable to launch an adequate rally, only moving up a very small amount. Others will start to lose momentum, which will be seen clearly in their quarterly earnings reports.

When you observe this pivotal point, some stocks will appear to be defying the odds and going against the trend giving a false impression of strength. What you are really seeing though is just a delay of what will inevitably come. All the stocks while eventually tumble regardless of what you might otherwise believe.

The cue to take here is simple. When you start to see a few of the market leaders begin to decline, it is time to exit your position. While others may appear to be stronger and can outlast the trend, don't be fooled. Follow the leader to the nearest exit if you genuinely want to protect your investment. It is better to wait on the sidelines with cash in your hands than to leave it to the bears that will slowly strip it away from you.

When to Get Out: When to Jump Back In

It is clear that the best time to get out of a bear market is in its early stages. The longer you stay in place, the more of your investment you stand to lose. But after you're out, you should still keep a keen eye on the market movements, constantly looking for a place where you can get back in the game.

The trick, however, is to know when to get back in. Once a bear market begins its downward spiral, there will be several rallies or attempts to recover, each one successively failing until the market finally breaks through the resistance and starts to climb again. You must be careful in this area as the upward movements can be deceiving. If you jump back in too soon, the risk of losing your money in another drop from a failed correction is highly possible. For that reason, you need to also learn the signs that the market has actually reached its bottom.

Finding the Bottom

One way to know that the market has reached the bottom is to continue to look closely at the daily general market averages. Every time the market attempts a correction, there will be some type of rally. It is best to wait for a market confirmation.

Each rally begins when the market average has a higher close after a major decline on the same day. So, the price may drop a few percent in the early part of the trading day but later in the day or the next day, you will see a recovery where the price is higher. When this happens, it is best to wait it out for a few days. By the fourth day, you can start looking for a follow through with a bigger gain and heavier volume. If the rally continues to this point, you can probably be confident that it is genuine, and you have likely found the bottom. In these instances, the market's volume should begin to see a significant increase so that it ends above average. In most cases, this is a sign of a confirmed rally.

Still, this does not mean that you should rush to get back in. It is merely a sign that you have the go-ahead to be the first to get into those high-quality stocks that show strong sales as they make the breakthrough on their resistance levels. It is therefore smart to exercise patience and observe the market for several days and then proceed cautiously.

Key Turning Points

There are several ways to identify when the market is turning.

• Key Averages Diverge: When the key averages begin to diverge, it is usually a sign that each of them is moving in a different direction. It could also mean that one index is moving up and another is moving down. This means that the rally may not be as strong as it seems.

• Check Psychological Indicators: True investors do not trade on emotion. They plot and analyze charts, reports, and graphs diligently to find the right time to enter and exit. However, many speculators will jump in and out on a whim. You can carefully analyze the ratio of calls to puts to assess the temperament of the people. If the volume of calls turns out to be greater than the volume of puts, one could assume that speculators are bullish in the hopes of an increase in price. If the volume of calls is greater, speculators are likely taking a bearish position.

• Observe the Federal Reserve Board Rates: Any changes in the Federal Reserve Board's interest rates can be a very reliable measure of a change in the market environment. As a general rule, interest rates tend to be a pretty good measure of the current economic conditions. Historically, three successive hikes in this rate usually are an indication that a bear market is beginning. Many of them ending when the market drops.

Your ability to evaluate the market well and interpret its movements is not just about finding the right place to get in or out of the market. It's a tool that can easily put you in a position to navigate the market and avoid pitfalls and danger spots that most novice investors tend to fall into.

This knowledge will keep you ahead of the market and see you through to great gains that up until now only the pros have been able to achieve.

Chapter 11: Cutting Your Losses

It is an easy and well-understood expression to "cut your losses." The advice can save many an investor from losing their shirt on a potentially failing stock. But ironically, it seems like very few tend to savor that advice. New investors are often caught up in the decision to HODL or cut their losses. They're not sure if the stock is going to rally or just wither away from the stresses of the market.

No investor deliberately chooses a stock they believe is going to lose its value to the point that it is worth less than it did when they bought it. It stands to reason that if you're investing in the stock market, you are expecting to increase the value of your portfolio.

Your objective is not to eliminate losses but to reduce your exposure to them as much as possible. So, if you've invested in a stock and it suddenly takes a downward turn, you're faced with an important decision. Your ability to know when to ride the wave of recovery or cut your losses will make the difference between an amateur investor and success.

Why People HODL

First, it helps to understand why people

choose to hold on even when all hope is lost. It serves as a reminder that the stock market is pure mob psychology at work. Often, even in the face of clear signs to the contrary that the stock is not going to recover, they still hold on. Then, when all is lost, they fail to realize that their loss was not the result of bad timing or poor research, but instead, it was their own behavior that was the trigger. There are several reasons why this happens:

• Unfailing loyalty: As you look at your charts, almost every stock will show a zigzag line that starts in the lower left quadrant and gradually rises to the upper right. Given enough time, most stocks will go up in price even in the worst of times. The hope that the stock will eventually bounce back and make an astronomical recovery is in the heart of all people. The fact that some stocks have made such a move gives them even more hope. So, even if there is a huge drop in value, they will continue to hold on tightly, waiting for recovery. Sadly though, many stocks that lose value drastically may never fully recover and regain their former highs.

• Pride: Sometimes, it's just pride that gets in the way. Unwilling to admit that they made a mistake can compel them to hold on, proving their point that they were right all along. They will say things like, "it's not a loss until I sell it," they continue to stubbornly hold on to their position.

- Neglect: When stocks are performing well, it is easy to log on to your account and watch the money grow, but when they begin to show losses, that same exercise can be painful. Even if only a few stocks are failing, it can bring down the returns for your whole portfolio and you get the feeling that the whole bag is not worth your interest anymore. They turn off their computers like they are turning away from the scene of an accident rather than going in and just getting rid of the bad apples. The losses continue to grow unseen until the entire portfolio grows completely out of control.

These and many more reasons are at the heart of capital losses for new investors. Making the decision to hold on is not usually based on any type of real logic and sadly, it can lead to disastrous results. It pays to know when it is best to cut your losses and move on to more promising ventures than to continue to hold on in spite of evidence to the contrary.

Realizing Your Losses

While getting into the market is the key to investment riches, it is just as important to know when it is your cue to leave. It is inevitable when investing in anything that you're not going to get it right 100% of the time. Even the most successful investors have experienced huge losses, how much more for the new investor just getting into the market.

Once you accept this fact, then you can realize how important it is to have an escape clause in your investment plan. The sooner you are able to realize your losses, the better protection you can implement for the rest of your portfolio.

Imagine that you are invested in ten different stocks and indexes. After a short while, you notice that three of your stocks are starting to erode and you're beginning to bleed money. But the other seventeen stocks are still doing well so you assume that it will balance out in the end. The problem with this thinking is that the longer the losers stay in play, the more of your profits from the other stocks will be eaten up. So, for every gain you make from your good decisions, you are losing a significant percentage to those stocks that are eating away at it. It would be much better to shed those bad apples earlier, so you can protect those gains that are doing well for you.

Stop-Loss Protection Strategies

Here are a few strategies you can try to protect your gains:

• 3 to 1: For every gain, you receive, cut your losses at a 3 to 1 ratio. So, if you are making gains at 25%, then you should cut your losses at 8%, which is 1/3 of the profits.

• Recognize when you're wrong: When the price of the stock drops below what you paid for it, chances are you've made a mistake. If the stock continues to decline, don't wait around in hopes of recovery. For each point it continues to drop, your losses are growing. You can figure out what you did wrong later. For now, it's time to cut and run.

• Recognize the loss when it happens. Some are of the belief that loss occurs only when you sell it but in reality, if your portfolio has lost its value, you've already suffered a loss.

Remember, all stocks carry a risk of loss. It takes courage to close the door and leave some of your hard-earned money behind. But, the sooner you learn to cut those losses and move on, the better for your portfolio and your future earnings.

Chapter 12: Taking Your Profits

It is a lot easier to sit back and watch your money roll in when you've made a good decision. But even in the area of profits, there are those investors that make mistakes. In order to take your profit, you must have a time when you are going to let go of your stock. The question is when. Some investors see the price inching its way up the charts and declare they will bail at the point when the stock reaches its peak. The problem with that thinking is that it is not always easy to recognize this point and they end up waiting too long.

Ideally, the best time to unload a stock is when everyone else wants to buy it. Even if you could predict the peak point and try to sell, chances are you'll be unloading it at a time when it is on the decline and you'll have fewer buyers looking to buy in. But, if you decide to sell when the stock is still very strong, and the price is still climbing, you'll have a much easier time of it, and you'll avoid getting caught in that endless cycle of corrections that comes after a stock reaches the top.

Have a Plan

When it comes to knowing when to take your profits, you need to have a plan. As a matter of fact, having a profit plan is just as important as choosing the right stock. Over time, you will develop your own set of guidelines for buying and selling but that does not mean you can't start with a plan from the very beginning.

Talk to any investor today and they'll happily give you their own personal guidelines that have worked for them. There is no perfect strategy to know when to sell and reap your rewards but as you grow in your knowledge and experience, you will quickly learn what works for your portfolio and what doesn't. Here are a few key points that will help you develop your own personal plan of action.

- Successful stocks, once they move out of their base on the charts, will move up as much as 20-25% before they start their decline. Deciding to sell at that 25% pivot point would save you from having to take losses when the price starts its natural decline.

- If the price rises quickly – sell quickly, don't wait for the 25% peak.

- Cut your losses at 8%.

- Reevaluate the stock after you take your profits to decide if you want to reinvest for long-term profit.

▪ Sell stocks that are slow earners and put the money into proven winners.

As you gain more experience, you will be able to compound your profits simply by knowing when to take your profits and run and when to reinvest.

When to Sell

There are two important points to keep in mind when it comes to selling your stocks.

▪ If you choose right, then your selling is easy.

▪ Avoid big-sell off periods.

When you see stocks sold in huge numbers, it may be the knee-jerk reaction of an emotional investor base. Always check your charts to see if big sell- offs are common for that stock so you don't get sucked into a trap. Winning stocks may have pullbacks from time to time, but they rarely drop below 8% unless you bought at too high a price.

There are a few telltale signs to look for when it comes to selling stocks and taking your profits.

▪ Get out at the first sign of trouble while your stocks have still earned you a profit.

▪ Look for the largest daily price run-up. If a stock has had a significant run from its base, and the close for that day is larger than on any other day, it usually means it is near its peak. It's time to sell.

• Look for the heaviest daily volume. As the stock is reaching its peak, the volume will increase. Usually on the day with the heaviest volume, it will be at or near the top.

• Look for the gap. If a stock opens with a large gap in price from the previous day after a run-up, this is referred to as an exhaustion gap. It's a sign that it is peaking.

• Climax top activity. If a stock's rise to the top is so fast and active, and it continues the activity for several weeks (a climax top), it means that there is heavy volume distribution with no real price benefits.

- Distribution signs. When there is an increase in daily volume but no increase in price, sell.

- Stock splits. If a stock has a run-up of 25-50% in just a few weeks after a stock split, sell.

- When there are more consecutive down days.

- Check the 200-day moving average. Stocks can be sold when they are 70-100% above the 200-day moving average.

- On the way down. By all means, if the stock price is declining, don't wait for a rally. Lock in your profits and sell to cut your losses.

- When you see a new high with low volume.

- When the stock begins to close near the low for the day.

- If you see an attempt at a rally but it is ineffective.

No matter what level of experience you have, it is extremely important that you learn as you go. While it is very important for you to do research and prepare when to buy a stock, it is just as important to do a post-mortem after you sell. You want to know what you could have done differently, how to rake in more profits, and what mistakes to avoid the next time.

When to HODL

There are times when it is okay to stay in the

market and ride it out. If for example, you choose to buy strong growth stocks, and you have developed a price target based on your research and earnings expectations for several years, then you will want to hold onto those until it reaches your target price.

This strategy follows the buy low and sell high concept. Still, there are a few steps that you'll want to have in between to make sure you're not holding onto a dud.

• Watch the stock's performance for a few weeks to make sure that it is behaving as you would expect.

• Follow the market closely and make sure it's following the general market movements.

- Chart a cutoff point on a graph showing the point where you will sell if it starts to lose money - a sell line.

- If it stops rising, do not let it fall back down to the original purchase price.

The reality is that you can't win if you don't play, and you can't play if you're not willing to lose. Still, you can cut your losses exponentially if you have a plan to reap your earnings whenever you can. Even if you expect a stock to rally, it is better to pull out in cash, wait for the rally to confirm, and then reinvest when it is more stable.

So, whether you are losing in the market, gaining profit or HODLing, it is very important that you follow the guidelines and have a concrete plan moving forward. These are the things that turn you into a savvy investor that will earn you the profits you've been looking for.

Chapter 13: Diversification

Investing in the stock market involves more than just putting your money into an account and watching it grow. There are a lot of decisions to be made. You not only have to decide what you want to invest in, how much to invest, and where to invest. You also have to decide on HOW you will invest.

One of the biggest decisions you will need to make is on how you will diversify your portfolio. Any investor worth his salt knows how important it is to diversify. This is a rule that not only applies to the stock market but in a variety of areas of life. You don't study only one subject in school, you don't buy at only one market in your community, and you don't date just one individual before you settle down.

The old saying, "Don't put all your eggs in one basket," is a very valuable lesson for everyone to learn.

In the stock market, it is one of the most important rules you can apply. Those who are only interested in one or two stocks may fare well, but when those stocks begin to backslide, they can easily take their money with them.

On the other hand, if you research one or two stocks very well and you can gauge the market correctly, you can do quite well with just those investments. Other investors may have their hand in twenty, thirty different options and because they have so many, will not research any of them well and may suffer losses because of it.

So, the question before now is simple: How much should you diversify? It is clear that diversifying can work as an insurance policy, but too much diversification can cripple your returns. You don't want your portfolio to be too large, nor do you want it to be so small that you are vulnerable to the natural fluctuations of the market.

A basic guideline to remember is the more you diversify, the less skill and knowledge you have to apply to your investment strategy. Ideally, to get the maximum results possible, you need to focus on the areas you know well and have the time and ability to follow.

So, what is the magic number? Again, that is for each person to decide but many experts suggest you have only one or two big profit winners and a few smaller options in your portfolio. If you plan on having a large portfolio, then choose four or five of those stocks in industries that you understand. If, by chance, another great opportunity was to present itself, have enough discipline to sell something you already have and replace it with the new stock.

Exercising this guideline can help you leave emotion out of the trade. Because you will have to give up something that is already proving profitable, it will impel you to take great care in researching a newer prospect before impulsively just jumping in. This will keep your portfolio manageable. As long as you use well-developed buy and sell guidelines, a smaller diversification can be just as profitable, if not more, than having thirty, forty, or fifty stocks giving you smaller, incremental returns.

Dollar Cost Averaging

This is easy to do if you have $50,000 or more to put into the market at one time. You can pick and choose your stocks and buy into whatever stocks you want. But if you're a person with a limited amount of cash on hand to get started, you may find it hard to pick and choose which stocks to invest in.

Now, more than ever before, buying stocks over time can be easily done, even if you only have a few dollars to get started. Many broker sites like Robinhood.com, Stockpile.com, and even larger brokerage companies like Charles Schwab and E-Trade are now tailored to cater to the smaller investor, eliminating trading commissions and allowing you to purchase even a fraction of a share if needed.

You can accumulate your shares over time by setting up a regular purchase plan, adding the same amount to your account every week, month, or year. This is pretty much the way your employer buys your shares of stocks in their employee plans. You can set the amount you want to invest on a regular basis and automatically purchase your shares accordingly.

One of the advantages of dollar cost averaging is that it evens out the price of each share. While one week the price may be a certain amount and the next time, it may be 10% higher or lower. This way, you never pay the highest or the lowest amount for each share of stock.

This plan does not work well for everyone nor does it work well for every stock. However, it is an option that allows you the option to get into the market much sooner, diversify your portfolio, and start earning a return much faster.

Accumulating stock is not the only reason you might not want to buy all your stocks at one time. By spreading out the purchases, adding a little at a time, you can still capitalize on market movements. If you're buying a particular stock at one price and then later, notice the price movements looked favorable, you could always add more to your portfolio. If you do this just make sure that the average cost of your different buys do not exceed a reasonable price so that you can still make a profit in the end.

How Long Should You Hold 'Em

Many new investors are caught up in the debate over long or short-term investing. Some advisors are quick to say you should ride it out until you get the price you want, and others will tell you to get in or out when the price is right.

The reason there is such a disparity between the two opinions is that it is a matter of investment style. What one person may be comfortable with may not be what you are comfortable with. And in the end, the real answer is not how long you should hold them because that will depend on the movements of the market. The real issue is if you bought the right stock, to begin with.

If you've done your research and prepared well for your investment, the time you hold the stock should not matter. As long as you follow the guidelines in your choice, the market will dictate when you need to get in and out of a trade. Some stocks will fare better on the long-haul while others will do well with the short-term strategy. Each stock is different and your decision to move will be determined by its own dynamics.

A Word About IPOs – Are They Worth It?

When it comes to diversifying your portfolio, you'll find that you have plenty of options besides just buying stocks. We've already talked about the index and mutual funds, independent stocks, and penny stocks but there are a lot more options to choose from. You don't have to limit your portfolio to these. There are many alternative investment instruments to choose from.

Initial Public Offerings are an option that seems to attract the eye of many new investors. They are often more appealing to those who do not have a lot of money to invest in. Everyone wants to get in on the ground floor of the next big thing. Who wouldn't want to be a fly on the wall when Google, Amazon, or Microsoft offered their first IPO?

Unfortunately, these kinds of finds are few and far between. While profitable deals can be found, the odds of finding one are limited. You will also have to deal with a number of restrictions. Some IPOs have restrictions on how soon you could sell if the business doesn't do well, which could leave you vulnerable. You may not be able to exit your position when you need to and end up going down with the ship.

Also, many IPOs start off underpriced in an effort to encourage more buys. This shoots up the price on the first day or two of trading, but then you will see a drastic drop that they cannot recover from.

It is difficult to gauge how well they will perform since they have no history of research. There is no way to tell their true value or potential. For the new investor, IPOs may not be worth the added challenges that accompany them. This doesn't mean that you can't purchase an IPO if you have the stomach for it but as investing in the stock market is already a risky venture for a newcomer; it is an area of the market that may best be set aside until you have accumulated more experience.

If you are looking for other instruments to diversify your portfolio, it would be better to look at the myriad of alternatives available to you. Consider convertible bonds, tax shelters, warrants, mergers, FOREX, penny stocks, futures, and the like. Many of those are much safer than the IPOs and can still allow you to enter the market and make the kind of returns that can help you build your wealth.

Conclusion

Thank you for making it through to the end of Stock Market Investing for Beginners: Learn How to MAKE MONEY Investing in Stocks & Stock Trading! Become a Stock Market Genius! Let's hope it was informative and able to provide you with all of the tools you need to achieve your goals whatever it may be.

This book was not written for the die-hard investor but rather for the average guy who just wants to try to put a few dollars to work to his advantage. There is no way we can learn everything there is to learn about the stock market from one book, but the hope is that this book will at least lay a solid foundation for new investors to launch a whole new lifestyle from.

Here, we've tried to give you all the basics, so you can go forth and trade. We talked about several important fundamentals everyone needs to be successful in the stock market.

▪ How to buy low and sell high so you can get the most for your investment dollar.

▪ We explained how there are no guarantees and you should only risk what you can afford to lose.

▪ We discussed the different earnings reports and other documents you should be familiar with when evaluating a stock.

- How to decide if you should trade long or short-term

- How to compound your investment so your wealth will grow faster

- How to value a stock

- How to watch out for fees that could eat up your profits

- And much, much more

As a new investor, you're entering turbulent waters but that doesn't mean you can't reap the same kinds of rewards as the more experienced investors. Here, you will learn the secrets to stock market success and hopefully capitalize on them so that you can move onto bigger and better things tomorrow.

Finally, if you found this book useful in any way, a review on Amazon is always appreciated!

Glossary

ADRs: American Depository Receipts used by foreign companies that trade in the USA.

After-hours Deal: These are deals made after the stock market closes for business each day. All after-hours deals are the date for the next business day.

Annual Report: This is an annual report provided for the shareholders auditing a company's businesses for the preceding year.

Ask: The price that owners of shares want to get.

Authorized Shares: The total number of shares a company is able to trade. It must be larger than the company's public float.

Averaging Down: When you purchase a stock as the price drops with the hopes that it will lower the overall cost.

Balance Sheet: This is a financial statement detailing all of the companies' liabilities and assets.

Bear Market: A market condition where the prices of the stocks are expected to fall.

Bearer Stocks: These are stocks that are not registered with the owner's name.

Bed and Breakfast Deal: This is when you

sell a share on one day and then repurchase them on another day. It's usually done to create a profit or loss for tax purposes.

Beta: A means of measuring the relationship between a single stock and the overall movement of the market.

Bid: The price you are willing to pay for a share.

Bid-Ask Spread: The difference between what one person is willing to spend and what the seller of the shares is willing to accept.

Blue Chip: Shares issued by larger and more reputable and established companies.

Book Value: The actual net worth of a company.

Broker: A person who makes trades for you for a fee.

Blue Chip Stock: Stocks from large industry leaders that offer stable dividend payments.

Bull: An individual who believes the price of a share is climbing.

Bull Market: A market condition where the prices of stocks are expected to be on the rise.

Buy: To actually purchase shares in a company.

Call: When an extra installment comes due on shares.

Capital: The money needed to set up a new business.

Capitalization: What the market believes the value of a company really is.

Cash Settlement: A certain type of deal executed for cash rather than for an account settlement. These are generally settled on the following business day.

Contract Note: A printed confirmation letter issued by a broker indicating that a bargain was executed.

Coupon: The interest amount to be paid for a fixed interest stock.

Cum Dividend: Shares that are purchased

allowing the buyer to receive the next dividend.

Dawn Raid: The act of purchasing a large number of shares as soon as the market opens.

Day Order: An order that is only good until the end of the day it is placed.

Day Trading: The act of buying and selling a stock within a single day, trades are made before the market closes.

Dealing: The purchase or the sale of a company's shares.

Debenture: A stock that is issued and backed by company assets.

Depreciation: Money that has been set aside to replace a company's assets.

Dividends: a percentage of a company's profits that are distributed to the shareholders.

Equities: Ordinary shares; those that differ from loan stock or debenture.

Exchange: The place where stocks are traded.

Execution: The point when an order to buy or sell a stock is completed.

ETFs: Exchange Traded Funds are like stocks, but they are traded on an index.

Ex-Dividend: A share purchased without the right to the next dividend.

Final Dividend: A dividend that is determined based on the company's annual results.

Financial Ratio: A ratio that indicates whether a business and its stock offering are healthy.

Forex: Stocks offered on foreign exchanges (can also offer foreign currencies).

Futures: A contract that grants the shareholder the legal right to buy or sell Indexes or Commodities at a future date with a price set today.

Going Long: Buying stocks with the belief that it will increase in value over time.

Good Till Cancelled Order: An order that stands until all the conditions stipulated are met or until you cancel it.

Gross: Interest paid without deducting any taxes.

Hedge: A means of insuring a stock against risk.

Hedge Funds: Accounts that allow you to invest your money in hundreds of different stocks held in one account.

Initial Public Offering: The offering of new shares by a private company when it goes public.

Limit Order: An order to purchase a share with a fixed price limit.

Liquidation: The act of converting stocks to cash.

Liquidity: The amount of effort it takes to buy or sell a stock.

Loan Stock: Any stock that has a fixed interest rate that does not have to be secured by an asset.

Margin: An account that allows an investor to borrow money to purchase the stock. The difference between the total amount of the loan and the actual price of the security is the margin.

Market Order: An order to execute the transaction as soon as possible.

Moving Average: The average cost of a share price during a set period of time.

Options: The right to purchase or sell a share within a specified time frame.

Ordinary Share: Shares that pay varying dividend amounts.

Over the Counter (OTC): A marketplace outside of the commonly used stock exchanges.

Portfolio: The entire collection of shares owned by a person or a fund.

Proxy: A person who casts a vote on behalf of another person.

Public Float: The number of shares that are actually available for trade.

Quote: The latest price of a particular stock.

Rally: an increase in the price of a stock or in the

entire market.

Secondary Offering: When a company's stock is performing well, they take the option to offer more shares in order to raise more money.

Sector: A collection of stocks that performs the same type of business.

Stock Symbol: An alphabetical symbol that represents a particular company on the stock exchange. Each symbol can be 1 – 3 characters.

Sell: To get rid of or to sell any shares that you own.

Stock: A share or an equity that gives the holder a partial ownership in the company.

Stock Warrants: An instrument that provides the right to buy more stocks within a specified time period. These are exercised differently from an actual stock option.

Trading Volume: The number of shares traded on any given day.

Value Stocks: Any stock that is trading at a price considerably lower than it's worth.

Volatility: The speed of a stock as it moves up or down.

Yearlings: Any bond issued for a 12-month term.

Yield: The gross dividend amount of a share in percentages

Getting a full grasp of these terms can be very instrumental in helping you learn how to work the market. As you can tell from the terms listed above, there are certain strategies you can take that can help you to get ahead of the curve. For example, setting up a limit order rather than a market order may not mean much when you're purchasing one share of stock, but if you're planning on purchasing 10,000 shares, it can make a huge difference in the amount of money you pay for a trade.

Remember, your key goal is to try to hold onto as much money as possible. This is the first step in building up your wealth. These are more than just terms to use when you are trading, but they are also concepts and a way to navigate the many technicalities of the market. They will come in handy when you're trying to decide what to do and everyone and his brother is trying to give you a piece of their own source of wisdom.

Understanding this terminology is a way of keeping you grounded in realities so you don't get overwhelmed by conflicting opinions about different stocks and their potential. For example, one person may recommend that you sell, another may tell you to HODL, and another may recommend that you average down.

Description

Investing in the stock market can be very exciting for the new investor, but it is riddled with dangerous twists, turns, rises, and declines everywhere you look. It pays to have a useful guide that will walk you through the most basic of steps and show you how to turn a little money into bigger gains.

Everyone can make a go of it in the stock market with the right tools. Through the pages of this book, even a novice investor will learn:

- How to prepare to enter the market

- How to value a stock

- Different ways to invest in stocks

- How to read stock graphs and charts

- How to use stock history in investment decisions

- How to know when to buy or sell

- And much, much more

The guidelines, strategies, and tips included here will teach you how to not just get into the market but to work it just like a pro. If you've long been curious about the wealth that can be gained from investing in stocks, this book opens the door and gives you an inside view of how to work the market to your advantage. The only thing standing in your way is just to get started. Download it now so you can launch a new future for yourself in stock market investing.

CPSIA information can be obtained
at www.ICGtesting.com
Printed in the USA
LVHW031007241220
675070LV00006B/274